the shipwreck of my soul

THE SHEPHERD OF MY SOUL

DIVISION OF THE SOCIETY OF ST. PAUL  alba house
STATEN ISLAND, N.Y. 10314

the shepherd of my soul

meditations for all

wilfred le sage

Imprimi Potest:

Francis Burkhardt, S.J. — Praep. Prov. Extr. Or.
Taipei, April 5, 1964

Nihil Obstat:

Donald A. Panella, M.A., S.T.L., S.S.L.
Censor Deputatus

Imprimatur:

✠ Terence J. Cooke, D.D., V.G.
New York, N.Y., November 23, 1966

Library of Congress Catalog Number: 66-27533

Designed, printed and bound in the U.S.A. by the Pauline Fathers and Brothers of the Society of St. Paul at Staten Island, New York as a part of their communications apostolate.

Foreword

In our work-a-day world which lays such heavy claims on the attention and energies of the average man and woman, this volume will serve as a stimulus to priest and religious, laymen and women to keep first things first and thereby insure ultimate success in their undertakings.

For those who have been fortunate enough to have made a retreat according to the Exercises of St. Ignatius, the following meditations will be a wholesome reminder of the extraordinary graces received at that time and the consequent obligation of being true to the generous resolves prompted by these inspirations.

THE SHEPHERD OF MY SOUL will lead its readers through verdant fields of considerations on the life and death of Christ and will offer them choice morsels in the way of practical applications of the principles contained therein.

Our fervent prayer is that those who use this timely book will be drawn irresistably to model their lives on the one Good Shepherd who knows each sheep by name and encourages it to go on to greener pastures.

Robert I. Gannon, S.J.

Introduction

This little volume is not meant to introduce you to the Good Shepherd. You already know Him well, but certainly you desire to love and serve Him more faithfully. Since we are all in this category, meditation is something essential for everyone. After all, you are not being introduced to prayer but you are being invited by Our Blessed Lord Himself to perform this important obligation to pray regularly...with greater love and devotion. Remember, the only real failure is the person who has failed to pray.

Perhaps you have also heard someone speak like this: "I've simply taken too much for granted. I haven't made the proper study of my faith and unfortunately have been rather remiss in the matter of prayer. I have made retreats from time to time and liked them very much and now I've come to the point when I'd like to have something of my recent retreat...be a part of my daily life." If such are your thoughts or if you have a kindred desire or aspiration, then these little meditations will be a daily means of increasing your personal love for Christ. And isn't this what you really desire more than anything else?

This volume is neither a commentary nor a substitute for the *Spiritual Exercises* of St. Ignatius. It is merely a little development of these same *Spiritual Exercises* for practical use today.

Unfortunately there are many who cannot make closed retreats, some are paralyzed, others are convalescing in hospitals and rest homes. For this vast group, the meditations in this little book may be helpful. Then too, there are many blind people who would appreciate having a meditation read to them slowly. Men and women confined to iron-lungs share their sufferings in closer union with Christ through prayerful meditation.

More and more Catholics today are saying the rosary. In this volume there are short meditations on each of the Fifteen Mysteries. They may be helpful in explaining the rosary to others as well as increasing your own personal devotion to our heavenly Mother and Her Divine Son.

May He bless you always,
Wilfred J. Le Sage, S.J.

Procedure

Mental prayer is the raising of your mind and heart to God in order to express to Him your allegiance, your gratitude for His many gifts and to ask Him for the necessary graces for yourself and others.

In meditation you apply the three powers of your soul to prayer. These three powers are the memory, the understanding and the will. Your memory recalls a religious or moral truth, your understanding considers the truth and applies it to your personal life. Your will makes the practical resolutions to transform this truth into action.

Mental prayer, or meditation comprises three parts, namely, the beginning, or preparation, the body of the prayer, and the conclusion. To begin a meditation, place yourself by an act of faith in the presence of God. Then reverently make the sign of the cross, not merely saying the words but with the sincere hope that the Holy Trinity will be glorified during your prayer. Ask God to help you make your meditation as well as possible.

Now consider the subject matter of your meditation. Your choice may probably be some part of Christ's life, or one of the Mysteries as we call them. Then by way of prelude, or scene, picture to yourself the time, place and circumstances. Place yourself in spirit as a witness or partaker of the event.

The body of the meditation is usually divided into several parts. It is not necessary to cover all the parts especially if your mind and heart reach the point that leads you to prayer. Prayer is the principal part of every meditation. By making sincere acts of humility, contrition, gratitude or love as your soul dictates...your innermost soul contacts God. Listen to His voice within your soul. Jesus is near you no matter how many distracting thoughts may enter your mind.

Conclude your meditation by thanking Our Blessed Lord for the many graces given to you. Turn also to our Blessed Mother in your concluding prayers thanking Her for interceding for you, and do not forget the guardian angel by your side.

Keep in mind that meditation is God's way of bringing peace and joy into your heart. During the trials and difficulties of daily life, He wants you to look upward, "Sursum corda"...lift up your heart! The person who keeps the joyful hope of heaven in his heart seldom has a sad moment here on earth.

The subject matter for the following meditations is divided into Four Weeks in conformity to the *Spiritual Exercises of St. Ignatius.*

Contents

THE SECOND WEEK *** *The Joyful Mysteries*

THE THIRD WEEK *** *The Sorrowful Mysteries*

THE FOURTH WEEK * * * *The Glorious Mysteries*

The Good Shepherd

God is present. After saying a little prayer that my thoughts and affections and entire soul may be directed to Him, I shall recall to mind some picture that I have seen, or one that my own imagination may supply. At this time I will try to visualize the Good Shepherd, and call this:

The scene:

> To picture the Good Shepherd standing beside a steep and rugged mountainside. He is bending down and lifting up a little sheep with His hand. It is one that had strayed from the flock, helpless and near a dangerous cliff (John 10, 1-19).

The petition:

> I will ask the grace to realize that the Good Shepherd has come to save a sheep otherwise lost. Because He loves me, He desires to save my soul.

"I AM THE GOOD SHEPHERD"

Above all other titles, why did He select this one in referring to Himself? In ancient times, the kings were shepherds. When not at war or deeply concerned in matters of government, they led their flocks and vast herds to pasture. Kings were pastors. And so it is with our Divine King. Why did He choose sheep as a symbol? Unlike other animals they do not have to be driven; it is sufficient to lead them. The Good Shepherd never forces anyone but He leads gently...."Take My hand...I understand."

Now in this meditation, Our Lord wishes to remind me that I am one of His chosen sheep. He is my Shepherd. Am I able to sufficiently appreciate His personal care and love for my soul? No, not in this life. Nevertheless I shall turn to Him now with childlike simplicity to learn more thoroughly the meaning of His Divine Wisdom. Only Christ could say, "I am the way, the truth and the life."

THE WAY

How important it is to have not merely a leader but an infallible leader. We know from daily experience how often people are misguided. Men too often mislead their fellowmen. History reveals the fact that entire nations following in the path of an erroneous leader have met with disaster and ruin. Against this background of human trial and error, the Good Shepherd stands with arms outstretched to welcome all mankind to follow Him. There is no mistaking His voice, "I am the way." Now as I ponder these sacred words, what other conclusion is possible except this one: Christ is my way. He is my only way. Human ways fail but not the Divine way. Now in my meditation I thank God most sincerely for my faith. I believe that Christ is the way. Grant to me the grace, dear Lord, to follow you step by step. I place my trust in Thee.

THE TRUTH

Although God desires my meditation to be personal, that is, an increase of grace and love imparted to the soul, He does not want me to forget others. Living in society we come face to face with similar problems. We are invariable seeking for the truth. The God-given gift of our intellect constantly strives for its object: truth.

If account books fail to balance, search is made for the error. Again, in daily life, parents continually look for one essential virtue in their children. Whatever the child may have done, or omitted to do, the parents want to know the truth. Likewise in our courts of justice, the judge and jury seek the truth. Now in matters pertaining to eternal judgment and salvation how tremendously important it is to know, above and beyond the realm of mere human opinion, the truth regarding questions pertaining to body and soul, life and death, punishment and reward. Christ alone can give and does give each correct answer. Here in my meditation, Christ my Good Shepherd wants me to realize more deeply the vital necessity of union with God. To coexist with God is to coexist with *Truth*.

THE LIFE

Christ came into the world to save the life of immortal souls. And those sacred words which He pronounced centuries ago are true today: "I have come that you may have life...." His meaning is clear. He has come to fill my soul with His Divine Life! How can I begin to thank Him for such a gift?

In the first place, human life is God's gift. The birth of a child is still one of the most important events of the day. From birth until death, doctors and nurses are continually giving time and skill in their most serious efforts to preserve and prolong human life. All manner of medicines and the latest scientific discoveries are used to this common end. Very frequently the life of a person depends on a blood transfusion. What joy for a generous blood donor to realize that he has saved a life! But our Good Shepherd came to save more than mere human life. He came to save the life of immortal souls, even to the sharing of His Divine Life with them. Jesus defined this higher life when He said, "I am...the life" (John 14, 6). And now in thoughtful prayer I turn to Him simply by making acts of faith, hope, and love. How much more deeply do I realize that nothing else in the world matters except to live with God in my heart...my Good Shepherd. And as I listen carefully, the truth of His words bring their joyful message to my soul: "My child, I have loved thee with an everlasting love" (Jer. 31, 3).

Conclude with the "Our Father."

A PRAYER OF ST. IGNATIUS OF LOYOLA

Dearest Lord, teach me to be generous. Teach me to serve Thee as Thou deservest; to give and not to count the cost; to fight and not to heed the wounds; to toil and not to seek for rest; to labor and not to seek reward, save that of knowing that I do Thy Will, O God. Amen.

PREPARATORY PRAYER
BEFORE THE MEDITATIONS

My God, I firmly believe Thou are everywhere present and seest all things. Thou seest my nothingness, my inconstancy, my sinfulness. Thou seest me in all my actions; Thou seest me in this my meditation. I bow down before Thee and worship Thy Divine Majesty with my whole being. Cleanse my heart from all vain, wicked and distracting thoughts. Enlighten my understanding and inflame my will, that I may pray with reverence, attention, and devotion. Amen.

FOUNDATION AND FIRST PRINCIPLE

Man was created to praise, reverence, and serve God our Lord, and by this means to save his soul; and the other things on the face of the earth were created for man's sake, and in order to aid him in the prosecution of the end for which he was created. Whence it follows that man must make use of them in so far as they help him to attain his end, and in the same way he ought to withdraw himself from them in so far as they hinder him from it. It is therefore necessary that we should make ourselves indifferent to all created things, in so far as it is left to the liberty of our free-will to do so, and is not forbidden; in such sort that we do not for our own part wish for health rather than sickness, for wealth rather than poverty, for honor rather than dishonor, for a long life rather than a short one; and so in all other things, desiring and choosing only those which most lead us to the end for which we were created.

—From the Spiritual Exercises

The End of Man

Man's origin and final end have been made known by the Infinite Wisdom of God. St. Ignatius called this basic truth of creation and subsequent truths, "The Principle and Foundation." We read of man's origin in the opening words of the book of Genesis: "In the beginning God created heaven and earth." He was not compelled to create any person or any thing, but He did so by an act of His Infinite Love. Among the works of His creation, God created man to His own image and likeness. Man's soul is a reflection of his Creator. Why was man created? Man was created and placed on this earth for a very definite purpose, namely, to praise, reverence and serve God, and by these means to save his immortal soul. This then, is the one definite purpose of life and the only reason for man's existence. We all have the same Divine Source and the same Divine End...God.

This fundamental truth has not been understood by the world at large. Christ came into this world to be the universal Teacher. Being Divine as well as human He could and did say, "I am the way, the truth and the life." And when He spoke of man's soul and his destiny, He did so with the knowledge of God. Many have not believed in His Divinity. Many too, have distorted His words. Materialism has been the enemy of Christ and His doctrine. Wealth, honor, glory, and power have been falsely made the end of life. If there is no eternal retribution, why not seek out every possible gratification and pleasure? This is the mentality of a world that has lost its sense of spiritual values. To such men, Christ told the story of the man who had gathered rich harvests into his barns, and in the midst of his opulence and worldly success he pauses to make this reflection, "And I will say to my soul: 'Soul thou hast much goods laid up for many years, take thy rest; eat, drink and make good cheer.' But God said to him: 'Thou fool, this night do they require thy soul of thee: and whose shall those things be which thou hast provided?'" (Luke 12, 19-20).

To stress the importance of spiritual gain over material wealth, Christ said very definitely, "What doth it profit a man to gain the whole world and to suffer the loss of his own soul?" The following considerations will show us the truth of His words.

I CAME FROM GOD

Where was I a hundred years ago, or much less? I was nothing. Now I may read the history of men, women, and events, of culture and travel, but I had nothing to do with all these things. Today I am witness to the sunshine, the place where I dwell, the family from which I sprang, the name by which I am known. Furthermore, I know that I possess an intellect, will, understanding and memory, namely, a soul endowed with these God-given faculties. Likewise I possess a body with wonderful senses. Now this existence of which I am aware certainly did not come from myself. My parents? They anwser in the words of the mother of the Machabees, "No, it was not I who gave thee mind and soul; it was the Creator of the world." God created me.

Why? God created me out of His pure love. Had He any need of my existence, or could I be at all necessary to His happiness? Certainly not. But God did create my soul by an eternal decree: "I have loved thee with an everlasting love." How grateful I should be to my Creator!

I BELONG TO GOD

I came from God, therefore, I belong to Him. He is my Lord and Master. By Baptism I was made His child, an heir to His Kingdom. He is my King; I am His servant. As a servant I pay homage to my King by praise, reverence and service. God is infinite goodness, wisdom and love . . . hence my praise of adoration and love in return. God is good to me, hence my sincere gratitude for all His kindness and mercy. Reverence implies knowledge and obedience. My faith teaches me to respect God and His Holy Name. My service of God implies doing His Holy Will in all things prescribed by the Commandments of God and the Church.

God has given to me all that I possess. If He took away my mind, what would I be? I would be on the level with the brute animals. If He deprived me of life and motion, what would happen to me? I would be a handful of dust. If He took away my entire being, I would be nothing. Consequently, of myself I am nothing. I depend upon God for everything.

If I own a piece of property I can do with it as I desire, namely, plant, lease, rent, sell, or sub-divide. God can do with me just as He wishes regarding my fortune, my health, my life. He has eternal dominion over me. I belong to God. He speaks with the voice of a loving Father, "Fear not, for I have redeemed thee, and called thee by thy name. Thou art Mine" (Is. 43, 1).

I WILL RETURN TO GOD

He alone is my goal, I am destined for God. I was not created for man, for an angel, or for myself, but for God. I was created for His glory, namely, to know Him, to love Him and to serve Him.

Now I am returning to God. Each year, month, week, day, hour and minute, yes, each breath that I take, is bringing me closer to God and His eternal Kingdom. This world is not my true home. I am just another traveler on the way. What is helping me on this homeward journey more than anything else? My *Faith*. Witness those who have lost the use of speech, hearing, or sight, others who are paralized, cripples...but what are these privations in comparison with the loss of a person's faith?

Before entering God's eternal Kingdom, every soul must be tested. My soul will be tested today. "Life is a warfare," we are told. What is the objective? There is only one great conquest; it is the final victory over the world, the flesh and the devil. The salvation of my immortal soul! For unless my soul is saved, nothing is saved.

This is the goal. What are the necessary means to attain it? In an ordinary battle a soldier needs: training, ammunition, food, clothing, medicine.... In the far greater battle for eternal salvation, we are all soldiers of Christ if we have received the Sacrament of Confirmation. Is Christ, our Captain, going to send us into battle without weapons, direction, food, and other necessary help? No indeed, He is going to give us everything we need.

Now in my meditation I may wish to know more about His campaign, His Divine Leadership and example. These will be found later on when meditating on the Kingdom of Christ. Here I must be content to realize the end for which I was created. I came from God, I belong to God, and I will return to God. Dear Lord, on this homeward journey please give me the help and courage which I need to fulfill your Holy Will.

Conclude with "Our Father."

The End of Creatures

From the text of the *Spiritual Exercises of St. Ignatius,* we read: "And the other things on the face of the earth were created for man's sake, to aid him in the prosecution of the end for which he was created. Hence it follows that man must make use of them in so far as they help him to attain his end, and in the same way he ought to withdraw himself from them in so far as they hinder him from it." Here we come to man's great test upon earth, namely, the proper use of creatures, and by creatures we include everything outside of God.

The scene:

> To picture in my mind the wonderful creatures which give to the world its beauty.

The petition:

I will ask God for the grace to use creatures as H
intended, and never to abuse them sinfully.

THE HAND OF GOD

All creatures are a reflection of the infinite beaut
of their Creator. They continually mirror His majest
and power throughout the universe. Indeed, "The heaver
pronounce Thy Glory." The sun, moon, and stars r
peatedly beckon us to look upward in gratitude towar
their Maker.

No one will deny the beauty of this vast country
America. Out on the open coast where the ocean sti
for ever and ever, always changing and always the sam
on the prairies where the grass grows and the crops ripe
to the full; in the lofty mountains and the silent deser
everywhere under this wide sky, the feeling comes...
Someone has been here. Someone has made this beautifu
for me. That Someone is God.

Indeed, God has not only created heaven and eartl
the living and non-living creatures, but He also preserve
them continually in existence and acts directly in a
creatures according to His own established laws. Go
always acts with a definite purpose. And the purpose
creatures is clearly expressed in the words of St. Ignatiu
quoted above. Now in my meditation, I will thank Go
for His infinite goodness and providence and ask for th
grace to ever appreciate the multiple works of creatio
reflecting as they do, the Omnipotent Hand of God.

THE HAND OF MAN

If I step into a church I am nearer to God. I will imagine myself inside a Catholic church. Out on the street there was noise and confusion; here there is peace and silence. Human hands have fashioned this home for God. This is a house of prayer, of adoration with an altar of sacrifice surmounted by an image of Christ crucified. The crimson lamp is burning above the sanctuary. Someone knew how much I needed this moment. Each one of these creatures, the altar, tabernacle, crucifix and lamp and other objects tell me that God's home has been made beautiful by the hand of man. I look at my own. Are they the helping hands that God meant them to be? Have they ever clasped the hands of the poor and needy? Would I love to hold the hand of my own child? Would I love to hold a chalice? Now I join my hands together in prayer, asking God that I may use them for His work. And with my hands, I offer my heart and whole self. Yes, Someone knew how much I needed this moment.

THE HANDS OF TIME

The tiny hand of my watch is a constant reminder that one of the most important creatures in my life is passing quickly. Time, is another of God's gifts which gives me the opportunity of doing good. Wouldn't it be a wise thing if I made a little check up on my daily use of time? How much time do I actually give to prayer each day? Do I make the effort to attend Holy Mass on time? Is there a definite time for the family rosary, or is the entire evening spent on watching television?

Here in my meditation I should pause to thank God

for His gift of time which has brought with it so many blessings to the present moment. How precious this gift for the living and dying! Just before death, a soldier in Korea wrote to his parents in New York, "I had time to say my prayers."

There is one part of my life always appreciated and never regretted: the time of retreat. It is during the quiet moments of prayer and reflection that spiritual values penetrate more deeply within the soul. A person learns to evaluate creatures for what they really are and to use them properly as a means and not as an end in themselves. The necessity for self control may take the form of a good resolution. Over indulgence in food and drink can be most harmful. Moreover, certain creatures which I know to be occasions of sin, whether it be a person, place or thing, are to be avoided entirely.

Since I realize that it takes the grace of God to use creatures properly, or to abstain from their use if sinful, I will turn to Him for the strength and courage I need. And I will also say a prayer that others may use creatures for the better welfare of mankind and not for the destruction of property and people. God is watching the hands of time, and there is much good to be done. He speaks to us through the words of St. Paul, "Now, is the acceptable time..." (2 Cor. 6, 2).

Realizing that it is truly the acceptable time, I will try to understand and appreciate a bit more God's goodness as revealed in His creatures. What a drab place the world would be without His flowers and trees. But there is so much more; the smiles and gaiety of children! See them at the Communion rail to receive our Lord for the first time. Who could comprend the happiness in the hearts of parents on such an occasion?

Now in my meditation I will endeavor to recall the marvelous creatures that God has given me to this moment. My devoted parents and friends who have shown me so much loving kindness. God has given me priests to guide my soul even from my earliest years. I remember, too, the good Sisters and their words of encouragement. And above all His creatures, He has given to me His own Blessed Mother, and Saint Joseph.

Since God has been so good to all of us, why is the world in such a turmoil of deceit and war? Why are so many homes broken up and children left without proper care? On reflection I realize that the world at large has fallen into degradation because men have turned to creatures for their own selfish gains and not as stepping stones to God. How many times creatures have been preferred to God Himself. And how important it is to remember that to criticize creatures is to criticize their Creator.

In concluding this meditation, I will turn to God as my loving Father, and thank Him for His goodness and mercy, asking Him for the grace to use creatures as He would have me use them, and in spirit join with our Holy Father, Pope Paul, and Catholics throughout the world in prayers for peace. May nuclear force, God's creature, be used for good, and not for human destruction.

Slowly pray the "Our Father."

Indifference

The concluding part of the "First Principle and Foundation" reads as follows: "It is therefore necessary that we should make ourselves indifferent to all created things, in so far as it is left to the liberty of the free will to do so and is not forbidden; in such sort that we do not for our part wish for health rather than sickness, for a long life rather than a short one; and so in all other things desiring and choosing only those which lead us to the end for which we were created."

The scene:

To witness St. Paul on the road to Damascus. He was converted by the grace of God, which prompted him to say in all sincerity, "Lord, what will You have me to do?"

The petition:

I will ask for the grace to understand and to practice indifference to all created things as a means of conforming my will to God's Will.

WHAT IS INDIFFERENCE?

The word *indifference* does not mean an absence of feeling, nor to be uninterested, as is often expressed: "I don't care." St. Ignatius uses the word with a very exact meaning, namely, as a state of soul by which we stand ready to do whatever God wants us to do. Now what is the relationship between this principle of indifference and the former meditation? In our last meditation we saw that we should make use of creatures when they help us and to withdraw ourselves from them when they hinder us from the end for which we were created.

There is only one way of insuring this control over creatures and that is to cultivate indifference, or detachment. The important point is this: creatures as a means to the end are not to be sought for their own sake.

God is man's final end depending upon his love, "Thou shalt love the Lord thy God with thy whole heart, thy whole soul, and with all thy strength." To reach this end, I must be ready and willing to choose the means. Indifference is an abiding disposition of soul. It has been expressed clearly in the above words of St. Paul, "Lord, what will You have me to do?"

We have the highest example of this supernatural indifference in the case of the martyrs. With the exception of miracles, they were not immune from pain, suffering and death. Their one desire was not to miss the end for which they were created. They made themselves indifferent to all else, and consequently *used* the creatures of pain and suffering to help them fulfill this end, and to withdraw from any creatures such as temporal reward or freedom if this would involve their consent to disown their King, Christ.

Today we have many examples of this even among small children in Red China. Thanks be to God.

THE PRACTICE OF INDIFFERENCE

The words of St. Ignatius explain the practice of indifference. "In such sort that we do not for our part wish for health rather than sickness...," etc. This indifference or detachment is a matter of the *will*. We are to make ourselves indifferent to the point of not wishing for one thing more than another. The result is that we make our will triumph over our preferences and feelings which are natural. How is this supernatural indifference attained? By mortification. Self with all kinds of desires and inclinations must be denied. Sickness or health, which do I prefer? Naturally, health. Supernaturally, whichever will help me to fulfill my end. Who will decide that? God. So if He does permit sickness, I shall know that it is the best for me. My will accepts God's Will.

One cannot reach this state of soul without having great confidence in God. He may not grant everything I want in this world; but He does give me everything I need for the next life. As tapestries are woven from the back, we see only the under side of God's plan, as Father Tabb writes:

> "My life is but a weaving
> Between my God and me.
> I may but choose the colors
> He worketh skillfully.
> Full oft He chooses sorrow,
> And I, in foolish pride,
> Forget He sees the upper,
> And I the under side."

THE REWARD OF INDIFFERENCE

It would be false to think that such a state of soul as indifference implies, is out of the question for me. God wishes me to live my life in accordance with His Holy Will. He will give me the necessary grace to do so. St. Paul became a great saint because he first realized his own utter weakness. Only after turning to God for help could he say, "I can do all things in Him who strengtheneth me" (Phil. 4, 13).

A little child at the point of death in China was asked this question by a missionary, "Now in receiving this sacrament of Extreme Unction, do you wish God to restore your health, or to take you to heaven?" The little girl replied simply, "Whatever God wishes."

And such will be my prayer now and throughout each day of my life. I will live in the hope that God will say to me, although so unworthy, as He said to Abram, "I am...thy reward, exceeding great" (Gen. 15, 1).

The world at large does not understand such a reward in future. They want only what *they* want, now. Consequently, mankind for the greater part has not sought and followed God's Will as a guiding light for progress. Man's puny will has been preferred to God's omnipotent Will...with the sad results apparent in so many parts of the world today.

Our Good Shepherd looks upon His scattered flock with patience. His voice is scarcely audible in the midst of so much confusion of earthly matters. He wishes to lead souls to peace, but who will listen?

Thank God for those who do. The Good Shepherd listens to family prayer. He knows the best way to help each member of the family no matter what their problem may be. There is no problem beyond His range of help. His call is to each individual soul. More attention to His call will mean more obedience to His Holy Will. And this is His plan for happiness while here on earth.

This is the grace I shall ask for through the intercession of our Blessed Mother. Mary received her call from God. We know how graciously she responed for herself—and her faithful children, "Be it done unto me according to Thy word."

Conclude with a fervent "Hail Mary," and "Our Father."

the first week

Sin

The Triple Sin

We have now completed the "Foundation" of the *Spiritual Exercises,* and we have seen that it contains the highest perfection. The following meditations will consist in developing the principles contained in the "Foundation." We have seen why we were created, why all other creatures were created and how we are to insure their right use. Now we are to consider what it is that prevents us from fulfilling our end and makes us neglect the means. Only one thing has such power, and that is...sin.

Preparatory prayer:

> The preparatory prayer is to ask our Lord God for the grace that all my intentions, actions, and operations may be ordained purely to the service and praise of His Divine Majesty. This little prayer is said before all the meditations. See page 19.

The scene:

> It is by placing ourselves in spirit at the foot of the

cross on Calvary that we can understand the meaning of sin.

The petition:

"To ask the grace of shame and confusion of myself, seeing how many have been damned only for one sole mortal sin, and how many times I have deserved to be condemned forever for my many sins."

THE SIN OF THE ANGELS

That angels committed the first sin is a startling fact. Perhaps we have thought to ourselves, how could they possibly have done such a thing? Imagine who they were, pure spirits created in grace and destined for eternal happiness. Their destiny was a gratuitous gift of God as it is for each one of us. How beautiful these angels, God's most perfect creatures, destined for His heavenly court!

At dawn we have often witnessed the beauty of the morning star. It stands above the horizon as a beacon of light to welcome another day. Lucifer was like the morning star, bright and beautiful in the splendor of his intellect, a masterpiece of God's creative power. Indeed, each angel was a masterpiece, and so fully qualified for the praise, reverence and service of their Creator.

But these bright intelligent creatures had to be tested. They possessed free will. They were created for a definite end, namely, to praise, reverence and serve God, and then to enjoy the Beatific Vision forever, which is a reward and has to be won. Just what the test was is not clear from revelation, although a pious tradition reasonably well supported by eminent theologians, among them St.

Thomas Aquinas, indicates it was probably the mystery of the Incarnation. Being creatures of keen intelligence they saw at once all that it involved for themselves. It meant that when the Second Person of the Blessed Trinity, took to Himself the nature of man, they, the angels would have to worship God in a nature, "a little lower" than their own. Lucifer and his followers failed in the crucial test, and refused to adore the God-Man in human form.

Then and there the angels fell through the sin of pride. The contagion spread. The battle cry of Lucifer, "I will be like the most High," may well have been the expression of his thought as we read in Isaias, "And thou saidst in thy heart: I will ascend into heaven. I will exalt my throne above the stars of God" (Is. 14, 14). In other words the proud and haughty Lucifer cries out, "I will not serve!" And this is the voice of one destined for the service of God, from a mind enlightened by grace. Other angels, we are told, took up this cry of rebellion and immediately a tremendous change took place. Their love of God turned to intense hatred; sanctifying grace was lost, and lost forever.

Because of one deliberate mortal sin, they were instantly, "brought down to hell, into the depth of the pit" (Is. 14, 15). There they remain rebels forever, bereft of all hope, beyond contrition and amendment.

Now in my meditation I realize the terrible consequence of mortal sin. Where pride and disobedience led Satan and other angels, sin could also lead my soul, into the "everlasting fire which was prepared for the devil and his angels" (Matt. 25, 41).

Some were lost, but more were saved. The faithful angels have received their eternal reward. The name of the archangel Michael, "Who is like God?", became the war-cry of the good angels in the battle against Satan and his followers. What a glorious victory! God will be praised forever by His loving angels. And now turning to Him in my prayer, I will thank Him for His goodness and mercy in placing by my side one of His guardian angels to watch and protect me.

THE SIN OF OUR FIRST PARENTS

We do not know how long it was after the good angels had been admitted to the Beatific Vision that God created man to fill the places of the rebel angels. God created the world, and then He created the first man and placed him into a very beautiful part of it known as paradise. God created man, "to His own image," giving him an end to fulfill and surrounding him with all the creatures who would best aid him to fulfill it. He was created as the angels were, in grace; he likewise possessed the preternatural gifts of immunity from suffering, sickness, concupiscence and death. His Creator gave him authority over all creatures. Adam was God's masterpiece on earth.

But Adam also had to be tested. He was created to enjoy the Beatific Vision, a pure gift of God, provided he was faithful in the use of his free will. God spoke these words to Adam to test his free will, "Of every tree of paradise thou shalt eat: But of the tree of knowledge of good and evil, thou shalt not eat. For in what day soever thou shalt eat of it, thou shalt die the death" (Gen. 2, 16-17). God reserved one tree for Himself to indicate that He alone and not His creature was the master. God had the right to impose laws; man had the duty to obey them. Consequently, by obeying God's commandments and through praise, reverence and service, the goal of eternal salvation would be gained.

Satan, the fallen archangel, was interested in the matter. If possible, he would prevent man keeping that one command, and thereby prevent him from attaining the Beatific Vision.

Eve is approached by Satan who asks the question, "Why hath God commanded you that you shall not eat of every tree in paradise?" It had never occurred to Eve to question God's command before. Eve should have fled from the very word, "Why?" But she did not; she remained in danger. She answered that there was one forbidden tree, "God hath commanded us that we should not eat; and that we should not touch it, lest perhaps we die." God had not said, "perhaps." Eve was beginning to doubt His word; she was already ceasing to praise.

The tempter was quick to notice her weakness. "No, you shall not die the death. For God doth know that in what day soever you shall eat thereof, your eyes shall be opened: and you shall be as gods, knowing good and evil." He was putting before her the same temptation which caused his own ruin: "I will be like the most High." She was now ceasing to reverence, or she could not have remained to listen to such blasphemy. She was beginning to disapprove of what God had done. God, she thought, was keeping something from her to which she had a right. Now her curiosity was aroused. What could it be? Pride is growing stronger every moment. How wonderful to be like God! To be completely independent! She was free to choose and did so. "And she took of the fruit thereof and did eat." At once the supernatural life of grace died within her soul.

Need Adam have followed her? No. He had his free will. What excuse did he make to God? "The woman whom thou gavest to be my companion, gave me of the tree, and I did eat." Adam preferred to please a creature more than the Creator.

What did *God* think of their sin? We can tell by the way He punished it. Adam lived nine hundred and thirty years expiating his sin by toil, sorrow, and suffering. God spoke to Eve, "I will multiply thy sorrows, and thy conceptions. In sorrow shalt thou bring forth children." All shall be tainted with Original sin, concupiscence, proneness to evil, sickness and death. We witness some of the results in prisons, hospitals, insane asylums, battlefields. All of this because of one mortal sin! And He who punishes is God, infinitely just and infinitely merciful.

Adam and Eve were expelled from paradise but not before hearing God's own merciful promise of crushing the serpent which implied a Redeemer. "I will put enmities between thee and the woman, and thy seed and her seed: she shall crush thy head, and thou shalt lie in wait for her heel." Christ would be the new Adam; Mary the new Eve. God gave *hope* for the world!

A SOUL IN HELL FOR ONE MORTAL SIN

Although we all share in the aftermath of original sin, by way of preparation for a meditation on our own personal sins, St. Ignatius proposes this consideration, namely, "the particular sin of some one person who for one mortal sin has gone to hell; and many others without number have been condemned for fewer sins than I have committed."

The matter for reflection here is obvious and serious.

If the terrible punishment of hell is imposed for one mortal sin, how great is the malice of sin! If I have ever committed a mortal sin, I have deserved God's just punishment of hell.

Now I will endeavor to make a comparison. Out of the one hundred thousand and more who will die this day, I will consider a man dying with one mortal sin on his soul. He is the same age as myself. We have both shared a good education, had good friends, the same temptations, joys and sorrows. In the supposition that we committed a mortal sin, we both deserved hell. He died unrepentant and I am still alive. In other words, I have the opportunity to cooperate with the grace of God. And what is my shame and confusion when I make a carparison with others! Yes, "many others without number have been condemned for fewer sins than I have committed." The implication is that they have been justly condemned, and I have been afforded the chance to repent. Certainly now is the time.

"Imagine Christ our Lord present before you upon the cross." How good and merciful He has been to me a sinner. Reflecting on the following questions I will give my answer to my King.

From my early years to the present time, what have I done for Christ?

Now in my present state of life, what am I doing for Christ? What does this meditation reveal concerning the condition of my soul?

Looking to the near future, what will I do for Christ? I will try to obey His Divine command to take up my cross and follow Him by keeping more closely united to Him through prayer and regular reception of the sacraments. And I will endeavor to be more grateful realizing that my Good Shepherd is near me. I will try to remember throughout each day: God is the Divine Guest of my soul!

What does this meditation mean to me? Besides the tremendous malice of sin manifested in the just punishment of the bad angels, and the just punishment imposed on Adam and Eve, there is for me a realization of what God thinks of my sins. But with this reflection, I must be keenly aware of His personal love for my soul. He has given me this day and this hour to approach the cross and to speak to Jesus Crucified. My prayer now—will be from my heart.

Personal Sin

In this meditation, we are to make a careful survey of our own sins. They are the only things which we may truly call our own. Each and every one of them is known to God. And we have already seen what He thinks of sin, the sin of the angels, the sin of our first parents, and that of a soul in hell for one mortal sin. We come now to this very personal meditation. It must be made calmly, without anxiety or trouble, because the sins we are going to review have all been confessed and forgiven. Doubt and anxiety over forgiven sin comes only from the devil. Why bring up the past at all? Because, after the meditations already made, we are better disposed to understand the malice of our own sins and to offer to God a deeper and more sincere heartfelt contrition.

The scene:

Again I place myself at the foot of the cross, for I dare not review my sins at any other place. It was here on the cross that Christ fulfilled the prophecy: "If your sins be as scarlet, they shall be made as white as snow" (Is. 1, 18).

The Petition:

I will ask for "great and intense grief and tears for my sins."

MY SINS

By myself, at the foot of the cross with Magdalene, I am going to call up in array all the sins of my life. Now that I know so much about God and about myself than I did when I committed my sins, now that I feel so much more sorry than perhaps I felt when I confessed them, I do want to bring them here again and lay them at thy Feet, my Jesus, and let my tears mingle with thy Precious Blood.

So I ask my memory to aid me in the melancholy task. I will think first of the houses and places where I have lived. As often as I recall some particular place, I think of some particular sins.

Let the secret story of my life loom up before me when I recall various places ... from my childhood to youth, and from youth until the present hour.

My duty to God from childhood on deserves my attention. How often did I miss Mass through my own fault? How negligent I was about prayer and going to confession. How little has been my praise, reverence and service of God.

My duty to my neighbor. My record of the past unfolds positive faults in word and deed ... harsh and unkind words, sins of discontent and avarice, through

selfishness...sins perhaps of dishonesty and impurity...
refusal to help others.

My state of life: single, married, the religious state?
What are the duties of my particular state? How have
I fulfilled them? Sins altogether personal to self? Yielding
to pride, jealousy and vanity? Sins committed through
human respect? One after another they pass before me,
my sins. Am I not ready to turn in confusion toward the
Figure on the cross and ask Him to hide them all in His
sacred wounds?

MYSELF, THE SINNER

I have reviewed my sinful life and I sincerely feel
shame and confusion, for I have realized that God Himself was present to witness each and every one of my
many sins.

Who am I who have sinned thus? In comparison
with the thousands upon thousands in the celestial court
of heaven, in comparison with all the souls who have
ever lived...millions of human beings in all countries
of the world, and all the millions yet to come...how
insignificant I am. After death who will remember me?
The greatest are not missed for long. Everything goes on
as usual without them...there just happens to be more
graves among the others. And so the world passes on.

I am just a speck, an atom, in God's creation, yet I
have dared to raise my voice to say to my Creator: "I
will not serve." What intolerable insolence! Let me
examine myself a little closer. What am I? A handful
of dust. If I pick up a handful of dust it is light and dry.
How the wind carries it off. Yet that handful of dust
might well be my body...tossed to the wind. What is

it? A tiny speck of dust might claim: "at least I am something." But I was nothing and God created me. Consequently of myself, I remain nothing. And yet I have abused God's gifts to offend Him, to sin.

I HAVE SINNED AGAINST GOD

I have seen who I am. Now, who is God? Even the angels in heaven could ask that question. Who is God? Infinite perfection, infinite wisdom, love, and power. Whatever we may say of Him are all so many words of expression. Who can know God, except God Himself. And I have dared to sin against God.

It would have been bad enough to strike another person, still worse to strike a priest. and far worse a bishop or the pope. But I have used my free will to strike against God to violate one, perhaps even several, of His commandments. "I will not serve." That is sin. Against Whom? Against my Creator, Who gave me my existence for no other reason except that He loved me and wanted me to enjoy the eternal happiness of His blessed in heaven. Not only did He form me out of nothing but, unless He preserved me constantly, every single moment of my life, I would go back to nothingness.

What is God to me? My redeemer. He who died for me, who went Himself into the battle to fight for me and who won the victory for me. And He really did this for me personally, and would have done so were I the only soul living. This is the God against whom I have sinned. What base ingratitude. And now I see sin, filthy sin, as something most terrible...loving self more than God.

What is God to me? My friend. He who has planned

every stop of my life for me. He who has given me every gift which I have, my parents, friends, even my very faith.... And in spite of all my ingratitude God still loves me, still forgives, still waits for me. The angels still take care of me, the saints still pray for me. I marvel at the patience of all these creatures who are treating me far better than I ever deserve. What is the explanation of it all? God's infinite mercy.

Looking at myself, let me inquire: what have I done for Christ? I have repeatedly pierced His Sacred Heart with ingratitude and contempt, frustrated His designs, squandered His Blood. What am I doing for Christ? I am meditating on the foulness of sin, of my sins. Am I sincerely resolved to avoid sin in the future? What ought I to do for Christ? I must completely cleanse my soul from all the stain of sin. I must avoid every occasion of sin most carefully. I must continually use the means of grace, confession, penance, prayer and Holy Communion.

Now I will leave all my sins and shortcomings, all my omissions and imperfections at the Feet of Jesus, and hide my confusion in His Sacred Heart.

"I will praise Thee, O Lord my God, with my whole heart, and I will glorify Thy name forever; for Thy mercy is great toward me, and thou hast delivered my soul out of the lower hell" (Ps. 85, 12-13).

In the conclusion of this meditation there is a three-fold prayer as directed by St. Ignatius. For the purification of my soul I wish to ask the grace for an interior knowledge and hatred of my sins. First, I approach Mary, my mother and ask her to intercede for this grace so necessary for my soul. And then with her—I approach Our Blessed Lord, and then with Jesus and Mary, I accompany them to the Father. In a spirit of humility and sincere sorrow I shall beg forgiveness for all of my sins in the name of the Father, and of the Son, and of the Holy Spirit.

Death

Death is the consummation of my life on earth; it is the last thing that will be required of me, the last of my acts of praise, reverence and service. Death is the final act for me to use in conformity to God's Holy Will, the final proof of my indifference.

Hell is only a possibility for me; death is a certainty. The thought of death is suitable for every place and time because there is no place or time which is secure against it. "In all thy works remember thy last end and thou shalt never sin." This meditation, then, is to help me to meet death calmly and with sincere confidence in God's mercy.

The scene:

I shall try to visualize my own death-bed.

The petition:

The grace so to live that death will find me prepared to die.

THE CERTAINTY OF DEATH

Man was not created to die; it is a punishment resulting from original sin. Had our first parents remained faithful to God, they would not have experienced death. But as one of the consequences of their sin "it is appointed unto all men once to die." There is nothing more evident than this fact. Daily experience teaches us that every living creature about us dies. The flowers of the field spring up, blossom, delight us for a time, but soon they wither and die. Every form of animal life follows the same pattern of birth, life, and finally death.

Many other things in the world are doubtful, but death is certain. Yes, death has come into our own families. Our grandparents, perhaps our parents, brothers, sisters, relatives, friends, the rich and the poor, the mighty and the lowly, the sinner and the saint, all must pass through the door of death. But the most difficult thing to realize is this: *I* must die.

If this fact is so certain, why don't I make a stronger effort to live a better life? As a man lives, so shall he die. Do I live peacefully, happily, patiently and with confidence in God? Now?

THE UNCERTAINTY OF DEATH

Where shall we die and when? A perfect figure of speech was spoken by Christ Himself: "Death shall come like a thief in the night." Only death is a thief that takes everything, all temporal goods, honors, pleasures.

Looking through the pages of today's newspaper we shall certainly find some who died when they least expected it, perhaps in a plane crash, fire, earthquake, explosion. Approximately one hundred thousand will die today. But this fact is not the important one, but rather another one, how many were *prepared* to die? Moreover, if I were the victim, and called by death now, am I prepared?

Often we hear it said, "Well, don't make the same

mistake again. You may be excused this time." But with death there is no second time. How important, then, is this little meditation. Now I realize how often the saints thought of death with profit to their souls.

CONSOLATIONS IN DEATH

"Though I walk through the midst of the shadow of death, I will fear no evil, for Thou art with me" (Ps. 23, 4).

This is the great consolation of death; the Master wants me. He has sent the summons that He is coming to fetch me. If I have a long, difficult and unknown journey to take, I naturally feel anxious and fearful about it, but if a friend who has already travelled by the same route comes to me and says: "Do not be anxious about the journey; I will go with you," all is changed, I have no more anxiety. This is what the Holy Viaticum is to the children of God. He who has Himself passed through the portals of death who has tasted death for each one of His children, comes and says: "Fear not, for I am with you." We really love Our Lord more than we realize; we come to the end of life to know this. All other loves have disappeared. We are alone with God. "Behold I come quickly and my reward is with Me to render to every man according to his works" (Apoc. 22, 12).

And so, when I see the little table prepared with the white cloth and the candles and the crucifix, I shall know that all is being made ready for the visit of my Shepherd. I shall turn my mind to my last confession, one more application of His Precious Blood, one more opportunity for generosity, love and contrition. If I have always used these creatures during life, how dear they will seem to me now. The priest has entered the room and I hear him say: "Peace be to this house and to all who dwell therein." Not mourning, sorrow, anxiety, fear, but *peace*. The Prince of peace is here.

"Ecce Agnus Dei".... As I raise my eyes, I see Him close to my bed. The priest says slowly: "Receive the Viaticum of our Lord Jesus Christ that He may preserve thee from the malignant enemy and bring thee to life everlasting."

But the Church has further consolation in store for her dying child. Christ's minister gives me the crucifix to kiss as an assurance that all that is to be done is in the name of Him Who died for me. Next the devils are bidden to depart and the angels invited to be present. This is done in the name of the Blessed Trinity and "by the invocation of all the holy angels, archangels, patriarchs, prophets, apostles, martyrs, confessors, virgins and all the saints." Then each of my senses will be purified by the Holy Sacrament of Extreme Unction... the Master's own touch by the anointed hand of the priest.

The next consolation will be the Last Blessing of the Church and the plenary indulgence. Holy Mother the Church imposes one condition which I must fulfill before it grants me so great a privilege. I must invoke the Holy Name of Jesus with my lips, or, if unable, in my heart. What other Name in life has been more dear to me; what other name in death could I desire to call upon? Now I shall ask dear St. Joseph, the patron of a happy death, for the grace to live a holy life and to die a happy and holy death.

At this moment what more do I desire than to have the holy Name of Jesus on my lips in death. As a man lives, so shall he die. Consequently may His holy Name be frequently on my lips, and always in my heart. With this meditation on death I now feel closer to the Sacred Heart than ever before. It was Your death, O Jesus, that gave me life! Slowly and with devotion I shall pray the *Anima Christi*.

> Soul of Christ, sanctify me.
> Body of Christ, save me.
> Blood of Christ, inebriate me.
> Water from the side of Christ, wash me.
> Passion of Christ, strengthen me.
> O good Jesus, hear me.
> Within Thy Wounds hide me.
> Permit me not to be separated from Thee.
> From the malignant enemy defend me.
> *In the hour of my death call me,*
> *And bid me come to Thee,*
> That with Thy saints, I may praise Thee
> Forever and ever. Amen.

The Particular Judgment

The meditation on death left my soul going forth from the body, assisted by friends on earth and from heaven and conducted by Christ Himself. Now I am to be judged by Him.

The scene:

To witness myself a sinner before the tribunal of Jesus Christ.

The petition:

I will ask for a salutary fear of the particular judgment and the grace to live always prepared to meet my Judge.

MY SOUL

"It is appointed unto men once to die and after this the judgment" (Heb. 9-27).

I will consider my soul which has gone forth from the body. This separation of body from soul is only temporary because at the general resurrection all shall be made anew. That will be the glorious resurrection of the body as we pray in reciting the Apostles Creed.

Meanwhile gathered near my lifeless body, my friends are praying for my soul. Even while they pray, I am being judged.

Of what does the judgment consist? The soul enlightened by a supernatural grace, sees as in a picture its whole life, even to the most minute details. The soul sees clearly the use it has made of the body and each of its five senses. How were these creatures used during life? The soul sees clearly the use it has made of itself, the intellect, understanding, will, and affections. How were these creatures employed while on earth?

The soul sees the use it has made of temporal goods. Each day and hour of life must be accounted for. How important is that creature of time?

Furthermore, the soul sees the use it has made of the graces received in the supernatural order, the Sacraments received, the crosses and adversity sent by the mercy of God. Now the cross appears in its true light;

I understand fully the meaning of the cross in God's plan of salvation. Did I accept my cross and make it my standard of life?

All the sins committed from childhood to death are present: faults, and omissions of duty, and the graces not cooperated with. Now I see the good I could have done, but through laziness or selfishness did not do. All of my good works appear also, but how many of them were done purely for God?

THE JUDGE

Who is He? "He Who was appointed by God to be judge" (Acts 10, 42). He is the Good Shepherd Who has been near me during life. He is the one Who has shown so much love; I am the one who has shown so much ingratitude. Although I have sinned so often, He has forgiven me times without number: "I absolve thee from thy sins, go in peace." The all-merciful, meek and humble Jesus will be my Judge. But these qualities of His character, which He showed to me during life, will be shown no longer. The time of mercy and pardon is gone forever; the moment of justice has come.

Jesus is my Judge. I am alone in the presence of Him Who knows all about me. In the light of eternity, I see myself as He sees me. Any excuses which I make for myself now, will vanish. God knows everything.

What joy shall be mine if I have died in the state of grace truly sorry for my sins. I am in the friendship of God; my sins are forgiven. His light penetrating my soul brings my entire life into clear focus. One look...and the judgment is clear. Perhaps it can be compared to the single glance of Christ toward Peter after he had denied Him. I too, feel the need of reparation to God, and although I am drawn irresistibly toward Him, there is still need of purification. That one glance from God is for me the beginning of purgatory. I accept it joyfully because it is His Holy Will. My Judge be praised forever!

PREPARATION FOR THE JUDGMENT

Now I thank God that the moment of my Particular Judgment has not come; there is still time for reparation and amendment. My entire life is not too long a preparation before the final meeting with my Judge. What I hope to be then, I must try to be now. The better I know myself and my Judge *now,* the better will be His judgment.

There are two rules to follow in preparation for my Particular Judgment. The first is given by St. Paul: "If we should judge" (1 Cor. 11, 31). How should I judge myself? Each evening my examination of conscience should be a particular judgment of the day. My Judge and I look over the matter. What does He think of that particular action, that temper, that uncharitable word, that duty neglected, that temptation listened to? He is looking at me through and through, and what sort of a look is it? Is it one of approval or disapproval? Disappointment? I will thank Him for His help during the day, and beg pardon and mercy for my sins and faults.

The second rule that I should try to keep if I want to be prepared for my Particular Judgment is given by our Lord Himself in the Sermon on the Mount. "Judge not and you shall not be judged" (Matt. 7, 1).

Do not judge others, be lenient with them, be charitable in thought and word, do not criticize or impute motives for the actions of others. If I am so ready to excuse myself, why not excuse others? Is it because I haven't learned to love my neighbor as myself?

This rule of not judging others, how wise it is! And to break this rule, how foolish! Not knowing the amount of grace that other people possess, how utterly foolish of me to judge them. "Who art thou that judgest thy neighbor?" (James 4, 13).

Now after considering these two rules, it is surely evident how much of my judgment is actually in my own hands at the present time. Even now I can picture myself appearing before Christ, His wounds, His Sacred Heart. And I realize that His judgment of my soul will be made in accordance with God's own commandment: "Thou shalt love the Lord thy God, with thy whole heart, with thy whole mind, and strength, and thy neighbor as thyself."

He knows me and He loves me. I am not lost in the crowd. He knows the clay of which I am formed; every thought is open to Him. He knows all my hopes and fears, my good desires, my weakness and faults. Not a need is hidden from Him, not a single pang pierces my soul without His knowledge. Nothing is hidden from the eyes of my Good Shepherd. I can tell Him nothing that He does not know. Now He wants me to do my part; small though it may be because true love renders it very precious in the sight of God; and when "the Prince of Pastors shall appear, you shall receive a never-fading crown of glory," and be counted among the redeemed "when He shall set the sheep on the right hand" (1 Pet. 5, 4; Matt. 25, 33). I pray for this judgment.

In my concluding prayer I turn to my Good Shepherd and beg His forgiveness and mercy.

Hell

God loves souls so dearly that He desires none of them to be lost. And if lost, what terrible consequences follow. This meditation is helpful as a safeguard to our eternal salvation, for if our love of God should sometimes prove too weak to preserve us from mortal sin, then a secondary motive, the fear of hell, should prevent such a terrible tragedy. We can, therefore, understand to some degree the message from God to the world through the Immaculate Mother of God to the three children at Fatima.

The scene:

I shall place myself alongside little Lucy, Francis and Jacinto as they gaze upon the horrors of hell.

The petition:

I will ask for an interior sense of the pains with which the lost suffer so that I may do all in my power to keep my soul and other souls from eternal loss.

THE SCENE OF HELL

Lucy describes what they saw and heard. I shall endeavor to see and hear it also: "A vast sea of fire in which were plunged all black and burning demons, and souls in human form. Raised into the air by the flames, they fell back in all directions like sparks in a huge fire without weight or poise, amidst loud cries and horrible groans of pain and despair which caused us to shudder and tremble with fear. This scene lasted an instant and we must thank our heavenly mother who had prepared us beforehand by promising to take us to heaven with her; otherwise I believe that we should have died of fear and terror."

Here is the testimony of an eye-witness and I must try to imagine what these children saw and heard. A vast sea of fire. It gives no light; there is nothing in hell but darkness and pain. Loud cries and horrible groans. Here is something worse than warfare. The groans and weeping of the dying soldier cease, but not in hell. The misery continues without the slightest hope of recovery. There is only one answer to those cries of despair: "Too late, too late."

Christ Himself spoke of hell very vividly in the story of Dives and Lazarus, the rich man and the beggar. The latter died and was carried by angels to paradise. The rich man also died and probably had a very elaborate funeral, but his soul was buried in hell. How he suffered by the sense of taste when he begged Lazarus for a drop of water to cool his tongue. He was suffering for the sins of his tongue. And now for a moment's reflection. What of my own sins of the tongue? It's not too late to make a resolution regarding my use of language.

If the sight and sound of hell is so terrible what must be said of the sense of touch? Among the greatest pains of sense is the one produced by fire. Therefore the rich man could only repeat: "I am tormented in this flame." And he could have added the word "Forever." Added to this torment is one which goes beyond description as far as the senses are concerned, the sense of smell. At one period in China the odor of burning bodies was so intense over a distance of two miles that all windows had to be closed although it was the middle of summer. There is only one conclusion: What must hell be like.

THE ETERNITY OF HELL

Here I shall return to the scene with the children of Fatima. Our blessed Mother said to them: "You have just seen hell." So it was not something like hell, something imaginary, but hell itself, on the word of the Mother of God. Have I the courage to take one more glance? Then the blessed Mother added these words: "Where the souls of sinners will suffer forever." That one word "forever" makes hell what it is.

Now I can imagine to some extent the thoughts of despair that must run through the minds of the damned. That awful sentence of the divine Judge never for an instant to be forgotten: "Depart from Me, ye cursed, into everlasting fire." Added to this a remorse of conscience that can never be corrected: "If I had only turned to God and begged forgiveness. If I had only turned to Mary. If I had only made an act of perfect contrition."

Thank God it is not too late to repent and to amend the future. Now I have the greatest opportunity on earth, that of attending Holy Mass. What is it that the priest says at a very solemn moment? He spreads his hands over the oblation and prays "that we may be delivered from eternal damnation." Again at the very moment before receiving the Body of Christ the priest tenderly whispers to his Lord, as I also should do: "Never permit me to be separated from Thee."

Now I realize the truth. If I have ever committed

one mortal sin, I have deserved hell. How merciful God has been to me a sinner. What shall I say to Him? And what will He say to me? Speak, dear Lord. "Whisper in my heart: I am here to save thee" (Ps. 34, 3). Indeed He is here to save me from eternal perdition. O how many times, O Lord, hast Thou forgiven me? Your Precious Blood has made me clean. Dear Jesus I turn to You in sincere gratitude for your mercy toward me a sinner, and by Your grace may I always do my part in saving souls from going to hell forever.

Tepidity

So far in our meditation we has seen that:

Man has an end to fulfill.
Creatures are to help him fulfill it.
Sin is a deviation from the end.
Death is a consumation.
Judgment is the proclamation of the end.
Hell is the consequence of not fulfilling the end.

And then for him, who by God's grace, has fulfilled his end, will come purgatory, a state in which souls are suffering because they have not fully satisfied God's justice with regard to their forgiven sins. Purgatory is a state of punishment for things left undone, for lack of reparation for sin. Why is it then, that even if we manage to save our souls, we shall still have to suffer for the stains left by sin? One of the chief reasons is tepidity. This meditation may help us to understand how great are the dangers and consequences of tepidity.

The scene:

I will try to visualize the Sacred Heart of Jesus addressing my soul: "Whatsoever you do, do it from the heart."

The petition:

I shall ask for the grace to fulfill His desire.

WHAT IS TEPIDITY

It is a condition of soul, not a single act of sin or imperfection. Why is a soul in such a sad state? It has lost heart. Love is no longer the motive it should be. We seem spiritually satisfied if we just seem to get by. Life becomes irksome because we think of all the things we have to do. They no longer appear to us as the things we love to do.

It is a state of carelessness regarding the occasions of sin, of just doing what is necessary to avoid mortal sin, but without taking the proper means to avoid all sin. Briefly, it is a state of mediocrity, without generosity. The worst part about a tepid soul is the fact that it doesn't always recognize its sad condition. Is there some way of telling just how tepid a soul really is?

There are degrees of tepidity, as there are degrees of heat. Prayer is the thermometer of the soul. If I am prepared to analyze how I pray, I am ready to recognize how tepid my soul really is. If I treat my prayer, my meditation, as though it does not matter very much and can easily be omitted, certainly I am tepid. On the other hand, if I sincerely admit that I am often overcome with distracting thoughts, but do make an honest effort to dispel them, I am doing what I should do. Again it often happens that despite a good preparation of the subject matter, prayer is dry, and there seems to be no profit at all. This is *not* an indication of tepidity. Spiritual activity proves that love and faith are present despite the fact that there is no particular consolation or affection experienced. The soul that fears tepidity is not a tepid soul.

Tepid souls:

Do things through dull routine.
Carry the yoke of Christ unwillingly.
Look for earthly consolation.
Indulge in useless reading.
Think only of self, ignore others.
Up one day, down the next.
Act from mere natural motives.
Confess without resolve.
Communicate without fervor.
Are restless and weary in conscience.

CAUSES OF TEPIDITY

There may be several causes of tepidity; these three are the most common.

A feeble will. This is a will that fluctuates and hesitates and remains undecided. It does not exactly say "yes" to a temptation, but it does not decisively say "no." It dallies with it, because it is feeble enough to allow itself to have an affection for what it knows to be wrong. A feeble will acts upon everything else connected with the spiritual life. Prayers are carelessly said or omitted altogether.

A love of self. If persisted in this, too, will cause tepidity. The soul knows that it should give up some particular fault or habit but makes no effort at correction. Or again, it may be that the soul is tempted continually to commit a certain sin, it is warned of the danger of letting this sin become habitual. Certain means are recommended to help the individual avoid the occasions of sin, but due to self love, these means are refused.

Neglect in little things. This is a third thing that may cause the soul to become tepid. The spiritual life is built up by fidelity to little things. Little seconds, little minutes, afford the opportunity for little prayers, little acts of virtue, all like so many threads of tapestry woven closely together to form the pattern of our lives. How much good can result from a little act of kindness! The reward will be given to him that is, "faithful in that which is least…"(Luke 16, 10). If our enemy, Satan, can get us on the road of neglecting little things, he knows we are on the road to tepidity.

THE REMEDIES FOR TEPIDITY

Prayer is the first remedy. This means to ask God for light to see my soul clearly. If my conscience tells me that I am tepid, the first thing is to acknowledge the fact with humility and pray for the grace to be fervent. Our Lord has said, "I will make the tepid soul fervent." I must never forget this promise of the Sacred Heart of Jesus.

Love is the remedy for all of our spiritual ills. The Sacred Heart of Jesus is ever longing and waiting for me to return to a more fervent life. The soul that truly loves is never tepid for it sees in each act of the day, a means of showing love and resignation to God's Holy Will.

I will turn to Our Lord now and ask for the grace to love and serve Him with greater generosity.

The Conversion of Mary Magdalene

The Good Shepherd loves all of His sheep, but the sheep have not always loved Him. He has a special care and regard for those who have strayed from the path of the commandments, and He calls them back to the fold by His grace. But His greatest concern is for the sheep who have not only strayed away, but who are apparently lost. Such was Mary Magdalene, a great sinner, but one who eventually recognized the mercy, forgiveness and love in the person of Christ. Through Him she has become the model penitent for countless souls.

The scene:

> To witness Mary Magdalene kneeling at the feet of Christ in the house of Simon, a Pharisee (Luke 7, 36-50).

The petition:

> To ask for the grace, through the intercession of St. Mary Magdalene, for a greater knowledge and appreciation of God's mercy toward sinners.

MARY THE SINNER

Our Blessed Lord came into the world for a very definite purpose. He tells us in His own words, "I came not to call the just, but sinners" (Mark 2, 17). He came to call the stray sheep and Mary Magdalene was one of them. Our Lord might have told a story about a prodigal daughter just as He did about a prodigal son.

But He foresaw that the true story of Mary Magdalene would never be forgotten.

Magdalene was publicly known to the people of her time as a sinner, and as such, a public disgrace. Her soul was spiritually dead and with this death she had lost her self respect. Undoubtedly she possessed exceptional physical beauty and was aware of it. But she made the fatal mistake of sacrificing a greater beauty, the purity of her immortal soul. In this state, the world would still see a very attractive person but when Christ looked at Magdalene, He saw the full truth. Although her soul was tainted with the filth of sin, the Good Shepherd beheld the contrary, a potential saint! And He wanted her to be converted and live, to be joyful and even cause heaven to rejoice. "I say to you, that even so there shall be joy in heaven upon one sinner that doth penance, more than upon ninety-nine just who need not penance" (Luke 15, 7).

MARY THE PENITENT

It was hard to believe at first. One day a gleam of light shone through the darkness of her soul. She saw Christ for the first time. Immediately there was change within her heart; it was the dawn of hope. And when she heard Him speak, that first ray of light became brighter. Mary believed in Him. As she witnessed His kindness and mercy, grace enlightened her soul toward the only path, the path of repentance. Indeed, Christ had inspired her love to the extent of making her ashamed of her past life of sin. The conquest of the Good Shepherd had begun.

Mary Magdalene had not only met a good person

but One that is Divine, the only One that could satisfy the longing of her heart and soul. Her heart had been created to love and to be loved. Now for the first time she began to understand the meaning of true love. Our Lord's command for Magdalene and ourselves is not new but it does require light and grace to obey it wholeheartedly. "Thou shalt love the Lord thy God with thy whole heart and thy neighbor as thyself." True love is wholehearted. "Love me, as I have loved you," said the Master.

Mary realized her foolish mistake, the one that could ruin her soul and mine...self love. Self had led to sin, but now she was ready and willing to abase herself in the presence of One able to forgive sin. Mary was truly penitent.

MARY THE SAINT

The rest of Mary's conversion follows the path of grace even to sanctity. Christ knew that her sorrow was most sincere, and He knows it today when a sincere penitent takes the first step toward the confessional. Mary's heart was thoroughly penetrated with the dreadful evil of her sins.

Here I shall witness the scene. Mary quickly enters the house of Simon unrestrained by shame or fear. Then having knelt behind the person of our Lord, as undeserving to meet His gaze or to occupy His attention, Mary assumes the attitude of a servant. She then bathed the feet of Christ with her tears. O sweet tears of contrite love! Our Lord would never be outdone in generosity and now He forsees the time when His feet will be nailed to the cross and bathed in blood. This He would do for Mary; this He would do for me, because He loves all souls so dearly.

There was no need for words. Every action expressed her love to the full. As her tears were falling in profusion over the feet of our Lord, Mary strove to wipe them carefully with the flowing tresses of her hair. Here was an outward sign of an entire dedication of herself; here was wholehearted love. Whatever vanity and worldliness existed before, now disappeared. Mary had performed an act never to be forgotten; she had cleansed the feet of Christ! And how beautifully He would purify her sordid soul. Behold her kiss the feet of Christ so reverently and then anoint them with the contents of the alabaster box. To climax this scene our Lord looked down at Mary. The Good Shepherd had found His sheep. Then she heard Him speak those calm words of complete forgiveness, "Thy sins are forgiven thee." Could this be true? Mary believed. Her last tears were those of joy. Yes, she had found her peace of soul at the feet of Christ. And this is the lesson for all of us. Later at the foot of the cross, she would understand to the full how much Christ loved her immortal soul. But He could see her even now, kneeling to the very end beneath the cross, as the words of Scripture were verified with the sacrifice of His Precious Blood. "Though your sins be as scarlet, they shall be made as white as snow: And if they be red as crimson, they shall be white as wool" (Is. 1, 18).

Now in spirit I will take my place with Saint Mary Magdalene at the foot of the cross. With renewed sorrow for my own sins, I will beg forgiveness, and pressing the feet of my crucifix to my lips, thank our blessed Lord for the many times He has said to me, "Thy sins are forgiven thee. Go in peace."

The Prodigal Son

Thus far in our meditations we have been considering the great and serious truths of our faith. These imply God's justice rather than His mercy. Now we are going to meditate on one who deviated from his end. We shall notice that the prodigal returned to himself before he returned to his father.

The scene:

> Read Luke 15, 1-32 and imagine our Lord telling this story of the prodigal son to a group of young people while you place yourself in their midst and listen.

The petition:

> Ask for the grace to appreciate more fully the great mercy of God.

THE PRODIGAL SON AT HOME

He had all that a loving and indulgent father could give him. He was the youngest and was tenderly loved by his father. All he had to do was to correspond to the love which surrounded him to be a good son to the father whose one desire was to make him happy. This was the end he had to fulfill and he found it too hard. "Father, give me the portion of goods which falleth to me." What is the matter? Perhaps his father was too old fashioned, his elder brother too exacting. He was independent; he wanted to see the world, to have a good time. Why stay home? A spirit of criticism has taken the place of the spirit of *praise* which used to make him, with childlike simplicity, regard everything that his father arranged as perfect. He is getting a little tired of his father, too, a little ashamed to speak about him to his new companions; he is ceasing to *reverence* his father. He now feels that he has outgrown any rules governing his father's house. They were all very well for a child, but he now seeks liberty and indepence. He is tired of being obedient; in a word, he does not wish to *serve*. Why should I serve, he argues with himself, I who am heir to so much? The "portion" is mine; I will ask for it. His father grants his request although he is sad to do so. As soon as the boy got the money he decided to get away, out of his father's sight, and so he went abroad into a far country. As his father bids him goodbye there is no word of gratitude on the boy's lips; he rushes away without even saying where he intends to go.

IN A FAR COUNTRY

It did not matter where as long as it was far away from his father and his home; his new companions would show him the way all too gladly. All went splendidly for a time; all was bright and glittering and full of pleasure; at last he was his own master. He was making friends by spending money lavishly, not thinking how foolish had been his former life at home. Now he is praised, admired. He is learning the worldly way of thinking that it cannot be wrong to do what you like provided you pay for it.

How does our Lord describe this life of pleasure? "He wasted his substance," wasted his father's gifts. It is the world which has taken his eye; he has forgotten about God.

At last there came a time when he had spent everything. Everything was wasted, and what is a life of waste if not a life of sin. All his former admirers disappeared, and he began to feel for the first time lonely and deserted. He began to think a bit about his home and his father. But in the midst of his musings something happened. A famine came and he realized that he had not even the necessities of life.

However, his real sorrow is remorse of soul. He had wasted his substance living riotously. This life of riot was a life of sin. Who cares what is to become of him? Does the world care? His whole life is one of wasted opportunities, of wasted talents, of wasted thought and energy.

Life was miserable. The world had taught him to ignore God, to neglect his soul, to forget prayer and to laugh at sin. But before he had been under the spell of the world for many months it had actually torn out of his soul every token by which even his own mother might have recognized him: his buoyant spirits, his merry laugh, his bright eyes, his healthy color, his manly bearing. Not only had the prodigal bartered God for mammon, eternity for time, soul for body and virtue for vice, but he had descended to the level of the brute beast. "And he would fain have filled his belly with the husks the swine did eat; and no man gave them unto him." The world only gives to get, and when there is nothing more to get from us it has nothing more to give. There is no charity. Everything went from bad to worse; and yet, all the while, God was calling his child, first by one trial and then by another, drawing him by His own means to Himself, breaking down all his pride and independence by humiliations and creating a longing in his soul to return to his father's house. In other words, to return to God.

THE RETURN

God is good and knows how to send blessings in disguise. The greatest blessing in the prodigal's life of riot was the treatment he received from his own set when the rumor ran around that he was a ruined man. Now he looked himself in the face for the first time. He realized the dreadful reality of it all. What nights of feverish restlessness, of conscious guilt, of remorse almost bordering on despair did the poor stricken youth pass in that outhouse near the swine. Despair was crying into his soul: Too late, too late. He wondered how men and women could have been so cruel to him. Now he realized the false front of their supposed friendship.

Once again he began to think of his father's house. "How many hired servants in my father's house abound with bread while I perish here with hunger." At last he saw things in their true light; his father's plans were the best, his own were nothing but base selfishness. How he wished he had the chance once again of living in his father's house, of once again showing his love by his dutiful service. His heart was already breaking with shame and contrition and he said to himself: "I will arise and go to my father and say to him, Father, I have sinned against heaven and before thee, and I am no longer worthy to be called thy son, but make me at least as one of thy hired servants." He is humble now; his humiliations have done their work; he feels that he is no longer worthy to be called a son. He is contrite now. I have sinned against heaven and before my father, and I must go and say so, however difficult it may be. It was only after prayer that he formulated this resolution and the very words in which he would speak to his father. His one idea now is *reparation* to make up for the past by a life of devoted service for all the pain he had caused his father. "Make me as one of thy hired servants." That's what he would say. Let me do anything if only I may have the joy of being with you and serving you.

The return to his father was not so easy. In fact, one difficulty after another presented itself. What does he hear from his companions now? Go back to your father? Impossible. Do you suppose your father would look at you? Why, he would be ashamed to own you. Look at those ragged clothes. And besides, you have no money for the trip. You'd be foolish to return. So counsel the world and devil. But their advice made no difference to the boy. If anything, it urged him on to his plan of returning, because he knew that his father did love him and would welcome him back.

It was not an easy journey, the way back never is. It needed courage and perseverance to keep his resolution. The *world* had tempted him; now the devil would take his turn. Don't you remember how far you came? If it was such a long and difficult trip when you had money, what will it be now that you are broke? Can you go along the road begging? Not only for food but for lodging? Impossible. And when you get near home, if ever you do, how your old friends will laugh at you. Can you bear such insults? Never.

These temptations were strong. And then finally came one that decided the matter, a temptation that came as the crisis. Surely the devil would get him this time. Your father wouldn't have you back in the house. Even if you returned safely, you would be thrown out.

But the boy knew his father better than that. How many acts of kindness and forgiveness he had witnessed in his father's house. And if his father had forgiven others, would he not forgive his own son? The very temptation was God's way of strengthening the boy's resolution, of quickening his step. There was one and only one idea in his mind. I must return to my father, no matter what the cost may be.

He realized that he was doing the right thing, and that conviction alone threw a glimmer of light into his soul. Though his poor feet were sore and his body aching, the world seemed brighter as he walked along. Nearing his home, his native air seemed sweeter, the trees lovelier than anything he had seen since he had left them long ago. Grandually the landscape became more and more familiar to him. He didn't have to ask anyone now which road to take. He knew every lane, every tree almost; this was the land of his childhood, and boyhood memories came flooding through his soul like torrents splashing water bringing with them a certain forgetfulness of self, of his rags, of his hunger.

At last he turned into the long road at the top of which stood his home. "And when he was yet a long way off, his father saw him." It was not the first time that he had stood at the gate and looked down the long road, for the boy who had forgotten his father. But his father had not forgotten him; every day, in fact, had found him at the gate straining his eyes to look for his son. Now he recognized him in spite of his rags and his beggarly condition. "He was moved with compassion" and came "running forward to meet him."

Sure enough, the boy saw the form of a man coming towards him closer and closer. Why was he running? What a question to ask. It was his father sure enough. In a moment he was in the arms of his dear father making his confession, saying as best he could: "Father, I have sinned, I am not worthy to be called thy son." But his father's love overwhelmed him; he could no longer bear the thought that he should only be a servant, so he left out that part of his resolution.

They went up to the house then, the master of the house walking with a beggar in rags and saying to his household: "This is my son. Bring forth quickly the first robe and put it on him." The robe of grace!

The father was in a hurry to reinstate his son, and he gave the orders one after another. Put a ring on his finger, and shoes on his feet. Prepare a banquet. Let us eat and make merry for, "This my son was dead and is come to life again; he was lost and is found."

Such is the story told by Christ Himself to manifest God's love for the penitent sinner. Is it possible to doubt His love after this? Oh, let no man or woman cry out: "Too late, too late." With God it is never late while there is life.

Am I that prodigal? Have I gone out of my father's house, the Catholic church which He founded? Have I been in the mire of sin and felt the awful pang of conscience telling me to "arise and go back to my father"? What joy awaits the sinner who returns to God. He, the Lord of the world, stands with open arms ready to welcome back his son. "My Father, if I have strayed away, please take me back under thy roof, into Thy house. For thee alone I was created, my Lord and my God."

THE
SECOND
WEEK

The Joyful Mysteries

The Kingdom of Christ

We have come to the Second Week of the *Spiritual Exercises*. At this time, our constant prayer should be to know, love and imitate Christ. To become more enthusiastic for our Teacher and Leader, and to have the courage to follow Him, St. Ignatius offers this preliminary meditation on the Kingdom of Christ, in reality the very heart of Ignatian spirituality.

The Scene:

> It will be here to see with my imagination the towns or villages where Christ our Lord preached to the people and to hear Him say: "If anyone will come after Me let him deny himself, take up his cross and follow Me."

The Petition:

> I shall ask for the grace not to be deaf to His call but prompt and diligent to accomplish His most holy will.

THE CALL OF AN EARTHLY KING

Let us call before our imagination the most noble leader, the truest king that ever lived. "He is chosen for this office by God Himself, one whom all Christians reverence and obey." He is liberal, kind, good and considerate of all. This king desires to lead a great crusade to conquer the lands of the infidel since these belong by right to the king. It is not for any selfish motive but rather the desire to give to the infidel nations the justice of his rule and the Christian religion. It is a noble and lofty project inspired by God Himself, and He calls all of his subjects and tells them of his desires and plans. "My will is to reduce to subjection all the land of the infidels." He does not ask for help, but leaves all free to decide whether they desire to come with him on this crusade. Here are the conditions: "Anyone who will come must be content with the food that I eat, with the drink and clothing I have; he must labor during the day and watch during the night, in order that afterwards he may have part with me in the victory as he has had in the labor."

Indeed this is a cause glorious and just. Victory is assured and only a coward would hesitate to take up the standard of his king and follow in the conquest. In reality, how many have pledged such loyalty to an earthly king! Napoleon was one example in the history of conquest.

THE CALL OF THE HEAVENLY KING

Who is He? He is Christ the King! This is the King who makes a declaration to all his subjects: My will is to conquer the whole world and all enemies and then enter into the glory of my Father. He too has a land to conquer. What is this land and where is it? It consists of the hearts of men all over the world. Are they not His by His creation, by His redemption? And are they not for the most part in the hands of infidels? Then comes his appeal: "Whoever, therefore, desires to come with Me must labor with Me, that following Me in pain he may likewise follow me in glory." "With me"—everything is expressed in that phrase; it is a summons to a close personal union with our King, to work through Him, with Him and in Him.

What does this partnership mean? It means: "If anyone will follow Me, let him take up his cross and follow Me."

The work is a great one and begins very near home. Each one who decides to join in the great crusade has to begin in his own heart and subdue the King's enemies there, before there is question of spreading His kingdom among others.

It is the purpose of this meditation, first and foremost to look within our own souls and see if our praise, reverence and service of the King are what He desires. Is there any inordinate affection, any creature whatsoever, that is tending to destroy God's kingdom within my soul? This is the question that we must ask ourselves. The world, the flesh and the devil are still the enemies of all.

There is no question here of whether we shall follow Christ. That decision has long since been made; but the question is, how closely shall we follow Him? There is no one who cannot follow Christ more closely than he is doing right now. In fact, our whole life, our constant striving for perfection, what is it except to cooperate with divine grace in following more closely the footsteps of our Savior?

One of the most important features of this meditation is not only to pray but to listen, to the voice of Christ within my soul.

He could say to each one of us individually: "My child, give Me thy heart. We shall fight life's battle together; I will be with you at every step; I know that the difficulties are great, but I shall be with you through every sorrow and temptation. When the world, the flesh and the devil rise against the purity of your soul, take heart for I have conquered these enemies. If you stand at my side, the victory shall be assured. When you are weak and weary of life, I will be the nourishment and strength of your soul. Should you stumble and fall, I shall lift you up again. All the circumstances of life I understand. If your life seems one of tiresome and monotonous labor, I worked as a humble carpenter for thirty years. If you are sometimes misunderstood, I was accused of blasphemy. If the good you do is unjustly criticised, my miracles were attributed to the devil. If you find it hard to forgive even your relatives and friends, I forgave those who put me to death. If your well-intended plans at times seem to fail, I was judged by the world to be the greatest failure that ever lived. Although I shall not give you whatever you want in this life, I shall give you whatever you need for the next. If you must kneel for a few moments to confess your sins, I hung for three hours on the cross to blot out those sins with my blood: "If your sins be as scarlet, they shall be made as white as snow."

What will be our answer to the King? He does not say "Go" but "Come with me." You will have as companions apostles, martyrs, virgins, and saintly men, women and children of all ages who have followed Me.

MY ANSWER TO THE KING

The young man in the Gospel asked our Lord: "What shall I do to obtain life everlasting?" Christ answered: "Keep the commandments." The youth replied that he had always done so, and apparently he was telling the truth, for our Lord looked into his heart and loved him, and wanted him as one of His own personal followers. But when asked to sell his possessions the young man turned away; the creatures of earth were preferred to their Creator. Is there any creature in my life that I prefer, or am I willing to follow the king? Certainly we know that His love must reign supreme in our hearts.

> "For, though I knew His love Who followed,
> Yet was I sore adread
> Lest, having Him, I must have naught beside."

Are we made ready, through His grace, to answer in the words of Holy Scripture: "In what place soever Thou shalt be, my Lord O King, there will thy servant be." What was good enough for Him shall be good enough for me. It is my will to imitate my King, even to suffer injuries and reproaches patiently because He did; to be poor, hungry and thirsty as He was; to live a life of self-denial and mortification because He did, for no other reason than that I love Him and want to be like Him. "Jesus, meek and humble of heart, make my heart like unto Thine."

The answer to this prayer is the cross. Is it sufficient to take up our cross and follow the King? *No!* There is something more that we must do. We are too prone to think that the culmination of virtue lies in obeying our Lord's command to take up our cross and follow Him, whereas, in point of fact, the climax is not reached, until, having taken up the cross and followed Him, we become as little children "for of such is the kingdom of heaven."

First, I shall turn to Mary and ask her intercession. Then, I shall come to the feet of Christ the King with a pledge of my fidelity to follow Him faithfully, with the help of His grace.

> Dear Jesus, help me to spread Thy fragrance everywhere. Flood my soul with Thy spirit and life. Penetrate and possess my whole being so utterly that all my life may be only a radiance of Thine. Shine through me and be so in me that every soul I come in contact with may feel Thy presence in my soul. Let them look up and see no longer me but only Jesus.
> —Cardinal Newman

This little prayer of Cardinal Newman carries with it the full impact of this meditation. I must be penetrated with this spirit of my King. "May He be so in me that every soul I come in contact with may feel Thy presence in my soul. Let them look up and see no longer me, but only Jesus." Such is the vocation of a true Christopher, a true Christ-bearer. In other words, I have been chosen to be another Christ! It is one thing to imitate someone; it is another thing to live his life. It is one thing to imitate the historical Christ; it is another thing to live *His life*, that is becoming one with Christ and His Mystical Body, having Christ live His life in me. He calls me now to just such a life. What will be the answer to my King?

The grace that I ask at present...is to be generous to His call. The answer to His call requires a touch of the Holy Spirit. O Holy Spirit, Soul of my soul, I adore Thee. Strengthen, guide, enlighten and console me. I promise to be submissive in all Thou shalt ask of me, and I promise to accept all that Thou permittest to happen to me. Only show me what is Thy Will. Amen.

The Incarnation

In the preceding meditation on the Kingdom we learned that one of the essential features in following Christ is imitation. In this, and the coming meditations we are to see and *know* what example He gives us for our imitation.

The scene:

After considering the meaning of the Incarnation, let us enter the little room where Mary listened to the message of an angel (Luke 1, 26-38).

The petition:

I shall ask for an interior knowledge of our Lord and the grace to accept with sincere humility all the circumstances of my life with a frequent prayer: "Be it done unto me according to Thy Will."

THE NECESSITY OF THE INCARNATION

From the Holy Scriptures we learn to what condition the world had fallen previous to the coming of our Savior. We read, "Therefore hath hell enlarged her soul, and opened her mouth without any bounds, and strong ones and their people and their high and glorious ones go down into it" (Is. 5, 14). Prior to the Incarnation these words of the prophet were fulfilled.

The general condition of the world was one of intense misery. The devil ruled men by their passions and lusts, which he encouraged them to indulge. He held them captive by the things of sense, by the allurement of the world, by covetousness, by ambition, revenge and hatred. Under the reign of Satan, man was hard and unfeeling, without pity and tenderness. The one thing they admired was physical power to dominate, and the one thing they feared was the helplessness of poverty. Their life was divided between pleasure and cruelty.

God had created the world. Now in His mercy, He would send a Redeemer. Therefore, Divine Wisdom selects a plan whereby the court of heaven and not the depths of hell may be filled.

God was not too late or too early in the help he brought to men. The Second Person of the Blessed Trinity was made man in the fulness of time, at just the right time, that is, to perceive how much virtue would die out even with the help of the Old Testament and with a fitting preparatioon to introduce the New Testament. The advent of our Savior was perfectly timed. The Jewish nation looked forward to one great event...the coming of the Messiah! By comparison, nothing else was necessary. The world must have a Redeemer.

GOD'S PLAN OF REDEMPTION

Man had sinned and thereby had offended the Infiite Justice of God. God's Justice demanded an Infinite reparation. But man's being finite could never make adequate reparation alone. Will God abandon man to his concupiscence, sin and hell? No, God is all-merciful. Consequently He freely decrees the Redemption whereby the Second Person of the Blessed Trinity would assume human nature and unite it to His Divine Nature as the God-man. Being true man, he could make reparation, and being God, that reparation would be infinite. This perfect reparation undid the sin, wiped it out in God's sight, and gave to man his wonderful *Hope* of salvation. When God wanted to make us one with Him, in this incredible mystery of divine wisdom He made Himself one with us. "He emptied himself taking the form of a servant" (Phil. 2, 7).

We can understand from the simple Gospel narrative that Christ did perform miracles. We read that He restored sight to the blind, health to the sick and even life to the dead.

These miracles were in the natural order, the physical. Now the Incarnation restored man to something far greater than eyesight, good health, or even life itself. It restored him to the supernatural order. Man had no right to this order: it is a pure gift of God. How wonderful is this mystery of the Incarnation! God became man that man might partake of His divine nature. "He hath given us most great and precious promises that by these you may be made partakers of the divine nature" (Pet. 2, 1-4).

It is through the sacrament of Baptism which gives the divine life, of Penance which restores it, and the Holy Eucharist which sustains it, that man has recovered his lost estate. All this has come to us through the mystery of the Incarnation.

We know something of the artist through the study

of his work; we know something of man through the study of ourselves; we know something of God through the study of Christ. The Incarnation was God's way of bringing a knowledge of Himself through the revelation of our Lord.

THE ANNUNCIATION

The First Joyful Mystery

After untold years of sin and misery in the world, there was only one human being whom the sin of Adam had not touched; one who had fulfilled the end for which she had been created, one who had praised, reverenced and served God perfectly.

God sends His faithful angel to Mary. Great arch-angle though he is, he salutes respectfully this village maiden who will soon be greater than himself.

Let us witness this scene and ask for the grace to know Him better, so that we may follow Him with greater love.

I shall place myself in spirit in the simple cottage and also listen to the voice that Mary heard. "Hail, full of grace," that is, sinless one. "The Lord is with thee, blessed art thou among women." Mary is troubled by this reverence shown to her by the angel. She is afraid. But he tells her not to fear, and explains to her that if she will, she may become the mother of the King, the mother of Jesus the Savior. Mary listens attentively but she cannot accept this offer for she has taken a vow of virginity and this is a sacred promise between herself and God.

Humbly and quietly she asks the angel how these two things can be reconciled. He explains that a special miracle shall take place enabling her to preserve her vow and also become a mother. "The Holy Spirit shall come upon thee, and the power of the Most High shall overshadow thee." Then he gives to Mary a proof of God's power and his own authority.

"Behold thy cousin Elizabeth; she also has conceived a son in her old age, and this is the sixth month with her that is called barren, because no word shall be impossible with God." There was nothing more to wait for. Mary answers the call of the King. "Be it done unto me according to thy word." God, the Son took His body from her pure flesh: "And the Word was made flesh." The angle adored his Hidden Lord and returned to heaven.

A girl of fifteen or sixteen welcomes the Word made flesh within herself. Her heart is thrilled at this proof of love. God within her! What humility in every detail of this great mystery! Mary in her little home was the center of the world. Meanwhile the King had taken up His abode. The very God of heaven hidden within the virgin's womb. And this for love of souls. This I shall never comprehend: God's love for my soul!

How aptly the words of St. Paul express this mystery of the Incarnation: "O the depth of the riches of the wisdom and of the knowledge of God! How incomprehensible are His judgments, how unsearchable His ways" (Rom. 11, 33).

The Incarnation is Jesus, the Good Shepherd, entering into our life and consecrating the life we live. It is a Mystery of His infinite love.

Indeed His ways are unsearchable. They were unsearchable for Mary; they are more so for ourselves. The moment of the Incarnation is infinitely beyond human comprehension. "And the Word was made flesh and dwelt amongst us." As Mary believed this fact was true, so do we. At this tremendous moment, God thought of *my soul*. In conceiving Jesus, Mary conceives all those who will be in Jesus. I am one of her children through the mystery of the Incarnation.

Now in my concluding prayer, I will thank God for this tremendous act of His love—the Word made flesh! He still dwells among us. My heart was created to receive Him. And He looks forward to my next Holy Communion with far greater love than I could ever comprehend. Jesus comes to my soul, not once but often, even daily. Through the Immaculate Heart of His mother, I will offer my sincerest gratitude to the Holy Trinity for this blessed Mystery of joy.

The Visitation

The Second Joyful Mystery

This contemplation brings to our minds a very important truth: our God is a hidden God, and yet his influence predominates in every occasion of life. In this particular mystery we find Mary the mother of God bringing Him into the home of Elizabeth, secretly. As events turn out so unexpectedly, God in his hidden way brings the secret to light with an unforeseen joy. Elizabeth recognizes the mother of God. Today the world at large is so sad and upset, because only a minority have recognized Mary as the mother of God and the Queen of Peace.

The scene:

Here I will witness Mary making the journey to her cousin and being greeted as a queen (Luke 1, 39-57).

The petition:

The same as in the previous meditation.

THE JOURNEY

Only to the humble does God reveal his secrets. He bade Gabriel tell Mary of the happiness bestowed upon her cousin Elizabeth. Meanwhile Mary remained at home only a short time to adore, alone and in silence, the hidden One within her womb. Then she set out for the village of Ain-Karim. "And Mary rising up in those days went into the hill country with haste." She would much rather have remained at home just at this time, but she did not heed her own personal likes and dislikes. When God put a good thought into her mind or suggested a particular service, Mary obeyed at once. It was her love that prompted this hasty journey. Elizabeth needed her. Each footstep along the mountain-path was a little act of love. Thank God there are such devoted women today who follow in the footsteps of God's mother.

Each nun going about her work of mercy is another Mary. In the hospitals, by answering a patient's call; in orphanages, by hurrying to the cry of a child; in the classroom, by her example to the little ones...we see the image of Mary. But especially in foreign lands, by making long and tiresome journeys through rain, mud, heat and cold to reach the sick and the dying is love manifest in every step. How often the Sister's thoughts must revert to Mary walking over a rugged mountain path, also tired, thirsty and footsore to bring help to another. And then, as so often happens, the missionary Sister's heart is filled with a joy that more than compensates for every step and trial of her journey.... She has instructed and baptized a dying pagan. She has saved another soul. Her heart is glad with the gladness of God. Here I should pause to reflect a little on my own journey through life. Is my object to bring happiness to others or do I foolishly seek my own?

THE VISITATION

After her long walk through the hill country of Judea, Mary approached the door of Zachary's house. Elizabeth was standing on the threshold as if expecting someone. Mary hastened towards her and greeted her cousin with loving words. But what was her surprise when the aged woman, instead of returning her embrace, sank to her knees and exclaimed: "Blessed art thou amongst women, and blessed is the fruit of thy womb. And whence is this to me that the mother of my Lord should come to me?"

Little did Mary realize at first what her visit meant to Elizabeth. "And it came to pass, that when Elizabeth heard the salutation of Mary, the babe in her womb leaped for joy." The grace which had first touched the unborn John, was now poured out upon his mother. This visit that so honored and overwhelmed Elizabeth had not been sought by her. She had not asked for this favor. And of course this made her appreciate it all the more. The same may be said of ourselves. Whether it be a sinner in need of conversion, or one who is striving for perfection, God comes to both alike without waiting to be asked. He goes before us, seeks us out, for the purpose of His visitation. And for this reason our appreciation, like that of St. Elizabeth, should be the greater. God has loved us *first*.

Visits are paid by God each day to the faithful soul; interiorly by His Holy Spirit and the inspirations of grace, exteriorly by His Word, His sacraments and above all by the Sacrament of Holy Communion. I could never appreciate any of these visits enough.

And wonderful to realize, God looks forward to my little visits to Him. Do I think of this while passing a church or chapel? The invitation is always present. And should I find myself alone with Him I am never less alone. Whatever is dear and good to my heart is dearer to His.

Today parents and teachers have serious reasons to be concerned about the future welfare of their children. What is the spiritual future of my child? In reply to this question whatever sacrifices are made for Catholic education are not too great. And for what specific reason? From the first day of school till the final day of graduation, each soul is given the greatest opportunity in the world... to visit God and to receive Him frequently.

THE MAGNIFICAT

Returning to the scene of my meditation I shall try to visualize Mary and Elizabeth standing together overlooking a peaceful Judean valley. What words could express the thoughts of these two? Mary's heart was full to overflowing. No longer could she keep back its burst of joy and praise:

"My soul doth magnify the Lord," she said, "and my spirit hath rejoiced in God my Savior. Because He hath regarded the humility of His handmaid; for behold from henceforth all generations shall call me blessed. Because He that is mighty hath done great things to me, and holy is His name. And His mercy is from generation unto generations to them that fear Him. He hath showed might in His arm. He hath scattered the proud in the conceit of their heart. He hath put down the mighty from their seat and hath exalted the humble. He hath filled the hungry with good things, and the rich He hath sent empty away. He hath received Israel His servant being mindful of His mercy as He spoke to our fathers, to Abraham and to his seed forever."

Elizabeth listened in silence and in awe. Mary's song of praise was the sweetest the world had ever heard...and it will sound throughout the Church forever. It is a prelude to the life and doctrine of her divine Son. God has ever exalted the humble. They are His saints. And that is what God desires of me. Frequently I should read slowly and thoughtfully this beautiful Magnificat of Mary. If so, I too will learn in my daily life to "magnify the Lord."

Now I shall turn to the Blessed Mother, offering my praise and love as did St. Elizabeth when she first proclaimed the mystery of the Incarnation: "Blessed art thou among women...."

I will conclude my meditation with this little prayer to imitate Our Blessed Mother:

> I pray that I may carry Christ;
> For it may be
> That someone would never know of Him,
> Except through me.

The Nativity

Third Joyful Mystery

Here we come to a familiar subject. You have seen beautiful paintings of the Nativity of our Lord. Now imagine yourself an artist and picture to your mind the setting. Then enjoy the company of the persons represented, Mary, Joseph and the Infant Savior. Watch the shepherds approaching. This is the simple manner of making a contemplation.

The scene:

Let us approach the crib of Bethlehem with the Holy Family on this Holy Night (Luke 2, 1-14).

The petition:

We will ask for the grace to know our Lord better, to appreciate His humility and to receive the interior joy that comes with His birth.

THE JOURNEY
(This part of the meditation is optional.)

We shall enter the little house at Nazareth and if possible into the thought of Mary and Joseph. They were
both looking forward to only one event, the birth of the
child. Mary had made a few simple garments for the
babe; St. Joseph had fashioned a little cradle. Peace
reigned in their simple lives. And although not a single
word is recorded in the Gospels of what Joseph ever said,
surely at that time he was most thoughtful of his young
wife, speaking to her with loving kindness, keeping silent
when he noticed her in a prayerful mood.

A casual observer, even a neighbor living nearby would
not have noticed anything different in the life of Joseph.
He went about his regular duties, and yet, if ever a song
was written in the heart of a man, it was within the
heart of St. Joseph.

Just at the time when happiness filled the hearts of
Mary and Joseph as never before, they are unexpectedly
given a trial. There comes a loud knock at the door. It
is a messenger from the Roman governor. After a sudden
approach, he tells them of the edict which has just been
promulgated by Caesar Augustus.

Joseph thinks of Mary. Surely in her condition it
would be impossible to make the long journey to Bethlehem. It was winter, and besides, her days were nearly
accomplished.

The edict must be obeyed. The names had to be
recorded by a certain date. To resist now would only
involve greater hardship. Joseph must go and it was not
suitable that Mary should be separated from her spouse
at this time. While Joseph had been thinking, Mary

had been praying. Was not God near to her? Would He not assist them in this difficult situation? Anticipating his own words, Mary turns to Joseph and says: "Yes, Joseph, we shall prepare to leave."

And now I shall accompany them on the journey. Going along with them, I think of the marvellous patience and submission of Mary and Joseph to the will of God. They were not merely fulfilling the obligation of a worldly ruler who had issued an edict; it was decreed that the Son of God should be born in Bethlehem. Every step of this journey is by God's divine will. Does God will disappointments and harships for those whom He loves? It was surely a disappointment to Mary not to have her child born in the little house at Nazareth where she had made all her preparations with Him and for Him. And now what a tiresome and difficult journey it is, when she is so little able to bear it. And Joseph in his anxiety about Mary wonders if he will be able even to provide necessities for her when lodging at Bethlehem would surely be difficult to obtain at this time. But there is no murmuring, no complaint. Why? Jesus is with them.

We are getting near to Bethlehem now and I watch St. Joseph inquire from house to house, always with the same reply: "No room." God offered to many that night the glorious privilege of sheltering under their roof the Queen of Heaven, and the King. Even if Mary had proclaimed her great dignity and the consequent necessity for shelter, who would have believed her? Never again would such an opportunity be offered to the people of Bethlehem. We are told by St. Luke that "there was no place for them in the inn." How often inspirations of the Holy Spirit come to me. They call for acts of humility, mortification and prayer. But because they are not attractive and call for some sacrifice, my heart remains closed, there is no room. Isn't this the truth?

Perhaps we have been accustomed to look upon this and other scenes of our Lord's life as a carefully arranged stage play. Joseph was to go from door to door, and each householder was to refuse, but all was to happen in accordance with a previous understanding. We should be careful in studying our Lord's life and in meditating on the various mysteries to dismiss this thought from our minds. It is true that all was foreseen, but it is equally true to say that nothing was prearranged in the stage sense. All things fell out just as freely and naturally as if God foresaw nothing. Joseph's asking was not make-believe; it was earnest and sincere. He asks with humility and accepts his refusal without recrimination. God's will is seen in each refusal.

How patiently Mary accepted His will. She was not admitted into the inn because Bethlehem was full, of foreigners and visitors, full of gossip and clamor. There was no room for her. Our hearts, too, can be like Bethlehem with no room in them for God. If Jesus is not to be found within human hearts, it means that He has been shut out.

Mary and Joseph retrace their steps through the streets, past the entrance to the city and out into the countryside. They reach a poor abandoned stable. At least, this would do for the night. How little did Joseph realize that he had just selected one of the most hallowed spots on earth. In God's providence this cave of Bethlehem was a very appropriate place for the birth of Christ. Joseph would not have thought it so before the event. But on reflection we can believe it to be so...only if we realize Who Jesus is. Being God, He was beyond the need of any hospitality that the world could offer. What He deliberately chose, He chose out of love for our souls. There was not the slightest worldly attraction about the poor stable, nor the fact of being the middle of December when He could have chosen some other season, nor the fact of His having poor parents when He could have had rich ones. There is only one possible joy that He could look for on earth, only one thing that attracts Him, one thing that calls for His love, and that is the hearts of the holy and pure. Even in the cave He found that joy in Mary and Joseph.

For the rest, poverty, abandonment and suffering, all of these perfectly became Him as God made man. Why? Because He was the Savior. He began to save us in a lowly crib.

How beautifully is the coming of Jesus put in these few lines:

> Now she to Bethlehem is come;
> No tapers burn for Him or her.
> Yet in her heart's ciborium,
> To angels' songs she feels Him stir.
> One star is eager for His birth,
> And to the manger at its nod,
> High priestess she, of heaven and earth,
> Enters to bring forth God.

THE CRIB

It was not the neat little cradle that Joseph had made and had to leave behind in Nazareth. No, it was merely straw piled up in a manger. But it was on that rough bed of straw that the King was laid. Let us look for a moment at that little babe, but only for a moment, for we should first kneel and adore Him. It is our faith that bids us do so. Here indeed is the living inspiration for the most skillful artist, because it is Christmas. Christ is born!

Only a few hours before there had been no room for them. Bethlehem had offered no welcome. But now, at this sublime moment, away from the tumult of the world, Mary the living ciborium, is bearing the pure Host, while a resplendent star has appeared overhead, like a sanctuary lamp over the sacred spot, and angel voices bring to earth their glorious hymn of praise: "Glory to God in the highest, and on earth peace to men of good will."

THE SHEPHERDS

It was not the great, the wealthy or influential people of Bethlehem that were invited to the cave. The most wonderful thing in the world had taken place and they knew nothing about it. And yet, there were some who were found worthy to be called ... poor, insignificant shepherds. Did our Lord have a special reason for calling them? Yes. It was not merely because He loved them. He had loved David who was a shepherd boy. But our Lord had another reason, for He foresaw that in time to come He would refer to Himself as the Good Shepherd. He called humble shepherds to adore Him. They were faithful to His call. "Let us go over to Bethlehem."

It meant that they would have to leave their flocks. What must we leave in order to go over to Bethlehem?

The shepherds reach the cave. And behold the scene we have already described. Perhaps Mary, the Infant's mother would like to know why they have come. Mary listens to their simple story. She always listens. They told her about the angel who had come and stood by them, about the exceeding brightness although it was night, and how terrified they had been. The angel had said, "Fear not, for I bring you tidings of great joy that shall be to all the people; for this day is born to you a Savior who is Christ the Lord in the city of David. And this shall be a sign unto you; you shall find the Infant wrapped in swaddling clothes and laid in a manger."

And then Mary pointed to the manger. The Infant Jesus is also stretching out His arms to me. He knew me at the time of His birth as well as He does at this moment. He is my Savior; I adore Him, I thank Him for this great gift of Himself. Be my Jesus now and forever.

I shall listen. What does he say to me from the crib? I do not hear His baby lips, but His heart seems speaking to me. Do not seek Me in riches, do not seek Me in pleasure. For you will not find Me. Seek me where the angels went, the shepherds, with My Mother—in a manger poor, cold, suffering. There you will find Me and there you will love Me.

Before leaving this blessed spot, I shall say a little word to His mother, to Saint Joseph, and finally to the little Jesus newly born for love of me. Dear Jesus, make me humble. As Mary held You in her arms, let me hold You in my heart. In return for this gift of Yourself, please accept my little gift, my heart with its love for You, now and forever.

THE COMING OF THE MAGI

Epiphany means manifestation. Christ manifested Himself to the Gentile world represented by the three wise men, the Magi, as they have been called. What exactly were they seeking? The wise men knew that there must be something more than mere human life. They were seeking the Divine and God's own light from heaven led them to the feet of the Savior. We, too, join them near the little Babe of Bethlehem, for here, and here alone, is Life, Truth, and Love.

Man's first inherent desire is for life. We are familiar, in some degree at least, with the modern medical means of assisting life in its earliest stages to the very end. From birth until death, human life has been man's greatest care. But we know that the life of man's soul, his spiritual life is vastly more important.

Man's second inherent desire is for truth. He wants to know the how and why of things. Even the child is eager to know what makes the wheels go round in the simplest toy. The older generation is seeking for the answers too. In this modern age, the continual search for the secrets of atomic energy show how intensely individuals and entire nations are seeking for the truth. Beyond the material elements of life, the wise men of old were seeking for the truth, and they found the answer in the Infant Savior. We, too, approaching the Child, will find the solution to all of our problems, doubts, and difficulties, because only God, who is Truth Itself, can give the true and satisfying answer to human hearts. Indeed, only God can satisfy the longing of the human heart for truth.

And thirdly, there is within the hearts of all, the ever increasing desire to love and to be loved. The child instinctively loves its parents. Within the hearts of men and women there is that love of spouse for spouse, of husband for wife. God wants love to reign in the family, and for this reason made commandments to insure His love within the family and towards one's neighbor.

The wise men of old found the reward of their long journey in Bethlehem where Love Itself was born. They found the most perfect family on earth, Jesus, Mary, and Joseph. They discovered here the meaning of life, truth and love. And these are the elements that give to each of us, our being, our personality and our final destiny. Let us join in spirit with the Magi and kneel before the Child, the Savior of the world. God will never be outdone in generosity. The wise men manifested their faith and good will by bringing precious gifts to the Savior. And in return He filled their hearts with the eternal gifts of the spirit, God given gifts of life, truth and love. Yes, they came to the new-born King, and learned Divine Wisdom, that God is the Source of Life, is Eternal truth, and everlasting Love.

Dear Jesus, this is the wisdom that my mind and heart ever yearns for. I too wish to offer Thee the gift of my heart, my love, and my life.

The Presentation

Fourth Joyful Mystery

Following the meditation on the Nativity of our Lord, we again approach Jesus in His infancy. The purpose of this meditation is to understand and appreciate more fully the submission of our Lord to the Law of God... and the humility of Mary.

The scene:

Picture Mary in all her beauty holding the Child in the temple of Jerusalem (Luke 2, 22-39).

The petition:

Ask for the grace of sincere humility and purity.

MARY APPROACHES THE TEMPLE

For forty days Mary had looked forward to presenting her child to God. She would place her Son under the yoke of the law by fulfilling the specified obligations. "When the fulness of time was come, God sent His Son, made of a woman, made under the Law, that He might redeem them that were under the law, that we might receive the adoption of sons" (Gal. 4, 4-5).

Mary, however, approaches the temple like any other mother. There is not the slightest display of her great dignity although she carries the Savior of the world in her arms. As she walks along the road, perhaps another passerby steals a second glance with the thought: what a beautiful little mother.

If the stranger could only fathom a little of the love in the heart of Mary on her journey to the temple. What sentiments might he discover in the heart of Mary? Certainly her heart is filled with gratitude and love because her Child is so close to her. That love is expressed in the glance which she gives to the babe in her arms. Even now she loves to call Him by His name.

HIS NAME

The Holy Name of Jesus was chosen by God. How beautifully it was made known to the world by an angel. And today we bow our heads reverently when pronouncing or hearing the sweet name of Jesus. This exalted name, meaning Savior, implies our eternal salvation.

How Mary and Joseph loved His Sacred name. How often this day in the temple and the days that followed they called Him "Jesus." And this, too, is my daily privilege. How do I make use of the Holy Name of Jesus? Could a Catholic mother ever sufficiently appreciate the honor of teaching her little ones the sweet name of Jesus? Could a Catholic gentleman be more loyal than in preventing abuse of the Holy Name?

THE PROPHECY (Luke 2, 28-35)

Imagine the astonishment of Mary and Joseph when someone approached who seemed to recognize the Infant in a special manner. "And behold, there was a certain man in Jerusalem named Simeon: and this man was just and devout, waiting for the consolation of Israel; and the Holy Spirit was in him. And he had received an answer from the Holy Spirit that he should not see death before he had seen the Christ of the Lord." Here I reflect that good Simeon lived only for the day that he might see his Lord, while I am given such a great gift in being able to receive Him frequently, even daily.

Guided by the divine instinct, Simeon did not hesitate. Approaching respectfully, he asked if he might be permitted to take the child in his arms. How well Mary understood this particular request. This scene gives me the courage to make my own requests to the mother of God, because Mary always understands. Again I look at Simeon as he takes the infant into his arms. "Then he took the infant into his arms and blessed God." And then, with heart overflowing at the fulfillment of his great desire, he utters the inspired words: "Now thou dost dismiss Thy servant, O Lord, according to Thy word, in peace; because mine eyes have seen Thy salvation, which thou hast prepared before the face of all peoples; a light to the revelation of the Gentiles, and the glory of Thy people Israel."

The emotion of Mary and Joseph was further increased by the appearance of another person. This was Anna, a prophetess. She had likewise been favored by the Holy Spirit. The most joyful moment ever witnessed in the temple now brings with it a future glimpse of sorrow regarding the child and His mother. Simeon cast his eyes in the direction of Mary and spoke the following prophetic words: "Behold this child is set for the fall and for the resurrection of many in Israel, and for a sign which shall be contradicted; and thy own soul a sword shall pierce that out of many hearts thoughts may be revealed."

Simeon was permitted by God to look into the future. In some degree, Simeon foresees the mystery of Christ's suffering and death, and foretells Mary's part in the passion of her Divine Son.

The revelation was made. Jesus would have to suffer, and His sufferings would be so great that His mother's heart would be wounded as by a sword. Mary accepts this knowledge with peace of soul. Again her heart was repeating: "Be it done unto me according to Thy word." Here in the temple a great drama of the world has just taken place. Mary accepts her sword of sorrow.

Now there is one duty to perform in humble obedience to the law. Mary went to kneel in the court of the women and a priest descended towards her. She did not give him a young lamb as rich women were accustomed to do, but according to the custom of the poor, two turtle doves or two pigeons; one for the burnt-offering and the other for a sin-offering. Mary, so pure of heart, so sinless, chooses to be just as other women. There was no need for her purification, but how much need there is for mine...constantly.

Here I have witnessed our Savior's first entry into the temple. Later He would come into that same temple to teach the people. Above all He would teach everyone to *love*. Now I will turn to Mary and ask for the grace of humility and a pure heart so that I too may love God more and more for making another temple for His presence—my own soul.

Teach me, dear Lord, to follow the example of Your mother. In this mystery of the Presentation, when Mary offered You, her divine Son to the Father, she also offered herself, body and soul. During the Holy Sacrifice of the Mass, I will always offer myself in union with your Adorable Sacrifice to our heavenly Father.

I will conclude my meditation with a frevent *Our Father*.

Flight Into Egypt

Like others, Mary and Joseph made plans for the future.

But God's designs for them differed greatly. They had not foreseen the birth of Christ in Bethlehem, nor had they any idea of escaping into the unknown land of Egypt. How different God's ways are from ours. He alone knows the future. Many human plans fail, the divine plan never fails.

The scene:

Let us join the Holy Family on their journey, mindful of each hardship and privation (Matt. 2, 13-38).

The petition:

The grace to obey God's designs upon my life.

THE COMMAND

We recall the history of the scene. The three Wise Men had come and offered their gifts to the King. But they are warned not to return to Herod, but to return by another way into their country. That night, when the three Wise Men were on their homeward journey, rejoicing that they had succeeded in finding the newborn King, Herod was wakeful and anxious, wondering what news the three visitors from the east would bring him in the morning. Joseph was lying peacefully asleep in the little house where all spoke of holiness and peace.

As Joseph slept, an angel appeared to him and told him that the child's life was in danger, that Herod was going to try to kill Him, and that he must get up and take the child and His mother and fly into Egypt. Flight—in all haste! Flight in the middle of the night; no previous warning; no time for preparation; destination and length of stay perplexingly vague; the child is still a tender infant; the mother requiring proper food and care. To mere human reasoning doesn't it seem all wrong? By a mere act of His Will couldn't God have provided very differently? Why should God be fleeing before a petty tyrant at the cost of so much inconvenience to His most devoted loved ones? But the seemingly impossible was the message of an angel.

What startling news to be awakened with. Egypt? He had never been to Egypt. How could they leave immediately? It was night; who would show them the way? Did Joseph consider the matter from the human point of view like we so often do? No. Prompt obedience was his answer. "He arose and took the child and His mother and retired into Egypt." That is the fact of the case. Were there any difficulties? What order of obedience is free from difficulties?

How does Mary accept this order? Joseph makes known the message. Does Mary say: "Why, you're dreaming. We can't make such a journey at this time of the year. The roads are poor. We haven't enough money to make that long trip. It would mean 180 miles on foot into a hostile country. Joseph, are you sure the angel said Egypt? That sounds strange to me. Better wait until the morning. What would the people think if we started off for Egypt in the middle of the night?"

Does Mary make these excuses or even doubt whether Joseph did receive this difficult command? No, she thinks only of God's will. God has spoken and she must repeat her former submission in these beautiful words: "Be it done unto me according to Thy word." The necessary preparations are made. Once again they are homeless, Jesus, Mary and Joseph. Is this the way that God treats His best beloved? What they are doing is done for love of us. Jesus as an infant again chooses the difficult way, the way of the cross, an exile.

THE JOURNEY

This is not the first time that we have accompanied Mary and Joseph on a difficult journey. On the way to Bethlehem, they would at least be going among their own people...but Egypt?

Let us have the courage to follow them, these refugees. Again, they must have begged for food and shelter. It was not pleasant, that trip across the desert, the burning sands during the heat of the day, the loneliness and uncertain shelter for the night. At times they became tired, thirsty and hungry. Those whom God loves so dearly as Mary and Joseph were not spared a probation, nor shall anyone. We, too, must expect trials of obedience, humility and patience. During this time God does grant the grace to carry on. And in the particular circumstances of this trip to Egypt, what a consolation to know that Jesus was with them. They, His creatures, had saved His life.

The sole object of Mary and Joseph was to keep and protect the child. Such is our duty upon earth, to keep Jesus always with us.

ABANDONMENT TO GOD'S HOLY WILL

This is the important lesson: Mary and Joseph abandoned themelves to God concerning everything; concerning their souls and bodies; concerning the time and place of their exile. They left their country, friends, and acquaintances. It was during the night, in winter, and they had no guide to lead them. Their one anxiety was to conform themselves to the divine will.

Are these my dispostions? Have I abandoned myself to providence? Concerning my body, food, health, sickness, life, death?

Despite their privations, Mary and Joseph were greatly consoled. They doubtless made the reflection: we will have to suffer in Egypt; we shall have no friends, but Jesus will be with us. He will share and sweeten our sufferings. Having Him with us, what can we dread. What more could we desire?

It is by this same abandment to God's holy will in this valley of tears, this exile, the midst of the series of disappointing events that make up life, that I will enjoy a foretaste of heaven, because abandonment will bring peace. Who possesses Jesus, possesses all.

Confidence is the virtue that we learn most effectively in this meditation. It is not that kind of confidence which makes us trust that God will do this or that, but the simple and profound confidence in what God *is doing*. It was this truth that prompted St. Theresa to say: "It is what God does that I love." And it is important to remember that God frequently does the unexpected.

Jesus is now an exile in Egypt. But He did have the consolation of not being alone. Mary and Joseph were His loving servants, and that, thank God. is also our privilege." In what place soever Thou shall be, Lord my King, there will Thy servant be" (2 Kings, 5).

Think of Jesus today. The world over an exile of love in the Holy Eucharist. O how many tabernacles there are! And I am one of His living tabernacles. Do I give Him the welcome in my own soul that He so justly deserves? Remember always the teaching of our Lord. He wants me to know that I am an exile here upon earth and He wants me to live that way and to pray that way. "And after this our exile...."

But there is something more in life than mere exile. We are never alone. Even in their exile Mary and Joseph experience joy which all the wealth in the world could not buy. For they have Jesus; they see Him grow and develop; they hear his first baby words, they guide his first uncertain steps; they gaze into his bright eyes; they are rewarded with His tender smile and outstretched arms to embrace them. Hardship was accepted for His sake. He had been saved. Egypt was not an exile devoid of love. Nor does God wish my exile here on earth to be devoid of His love. Like Mary and Joseph, I too, have been chosen to labor, to suffer, and to serve Him. But a service of *love* makes all the difference in the world. And such service shall not be without its eternal reward. In conclusion I will pray the *Hail Holy Queen:* "And after this our exile show unto us the blessed fruit of thy womb, Jesus."

Finding of the Child Jesus

Fifth Joyful Mystery

In this meditation we learn that the joy of finding the child followed the sorrow of the loss of the child. God's plan of joy and sorrow is likewise interwoven in our own lives. What we imagine to be a loss, often enough in God's plan may not be a loss at all but rather a blessing in disguise. Our Blessed Lord brought joy into the hearts of Mary and Joseph by manifesting to them His own divine missions, as He said, "My Father's business."

The scene:

> Picture to yourself the beautiful painting of Christ as a boy among the doctors in the temple. "They found Him in the temple, sitting in the midst of the doctors, hearing them and asking them questions" (Luke 2, 41-52).

The petition:

> I will ask "for the grace of an interior knowledge of our Lord Who for me is made man, that I may the more love and follow Him."

THE JOURNEY TO JERUSALEM

The Paschal feast was always a feast of joy, but this year it was especially so for the Holy Family. Jesus would accompany His parents to Jerusalem. Joseph once again "took the child and His mother." How often had Joseph looked forward to this glad day as he had gone on his lonely pilgrimages previously. His humble soul is filled with consolation. What can we say of the joy within the heart of Mary? Whether we think of her on the journey rejoicing in the beauty of her Divine Son, or kneeling in the temple beside Him, her heart is filled with peace and joy.

Jesus is recognized as a man now under the law, and as the perfect Man He was keeping the laws of His Father. He had come to do His Will and He rejoiced to do it. He could not assist at His first Paschal feast without thinking of the one when He Himself would be the Lamb of sacrifice. He is thinking of us and even as a boy of twelve He desires to teach us that nothing else matters except the Will of His Father, the Will of God.

During the great Paschal feast Jesus looks at the lamb slain for sacrifice. He takes notice of the unleavened bread. But, in His mind, the lamb and the bread are only symbols of a far greater sacrifice to come. One day in the future He will be the Victim of Sacrifice, on Calvary, and today the Food of my soul. Dear Lord, continue to teach me of Your love.

THE LOSS

"When, the Feast being over, Mary and Joseph returned, the child Jesus remained in Jerusalem." What a strange thing. "His parents knew it not" till the two groups, the men and women met together at the end of the first day's journey. Each was longing to see Jesus again. Imagine the sudden sorrow cast upon them. It is as impossible for us to understand the desolation that chilled Mary's heart, as it was to understand her former state of consolation. We know that her grief was so intense that the three days' loss is one of the seven swords that pierced her heart and made her the Mother of Sorrows. Mary must learn the anguish of soul regarding those who have lost Him by sin. That is why her intercession is so great for sinners. It is important to note how our Blessed Mother acted during the absence of her son...that I may know how to conduct myself during the time of desolation.

Mary and Joseph spent long hours in search of the child. Most likely they both reproached themselves with carelessness in not making certain that He was in company with His mother or foster father. But one thing is certain; Mary and Joseph prayed to find their child. They kept searching. Today many are searching for Christ. Perhaps there is someone that I can help.

"Not finding Him, they returned to Jerusalem seeking Him." Their anguish was increased now as they revisited all the places where they had been with Him, the temple where they had knelt togther, the houses of the poor and sick to whom He had loved to minister. One question they ask repeatedly: "Have you seen Him, a young boy, our son?" Three days were spent in fruitless search. But was it fruitless? Was not each moment increasing the love in His Mother's heart and that of Joseph?

THE FINDING OF JESUS

Where was Jesus found? In the temple. He was probably in the temple when Mary first went to look, but it was not yet time to show Himself. He could gauge both her consolation and desolation, and He could have prevented all of her sorrow and pain had He so willed.

God's will is always for the best, but how poorly it is understood on our part.

"They found Him in the temple sitting in the midst of the doctors, hearing them and asking them questions; and seeing Him they wondered." Wondered at His wisdom, yes, but also at the calm way in which He was sitting there as though He had caused them no trouble.

It was so unlike Him. His Mother, with the holy familiarity which comes from a great love, reproached Him: "Son, why hast Thou done so to us? Behold, thy father and I have sought Thee sorrowing." Does not each word tell of their love? Our Lord knew that they had sought Him and He answered: "Did you not know that I must be about my Father's business?" And He had been doing it, even within the heart of His mother. "They understood not the word that He spoke to them." From this trial in the life of Mary and Joseph, we too, may take heart in this fact: An absent Jesus is not a lost Jesus.

They did not understand then that sorrow is the pathway to joy. Our Lord was preparing His Mother for the cross. He now speaks of "His Father's business" but one day she would hear from His lips those last words: "I have finished the work that thou gavest Me to do."

He wished also to give an example to those many followers of His who would have to go through the agony of leaving father and mother in order to do their "Father's business," by working for the salvation of souls. He would comfort them by bearing this trial first Himself.

How often a great mistake has been made on the part of parents who deliberately and without any reason, except selfishness, oppose their child's vocation to serve God. On the other hand, how often has God called a young man or woman into His service and found unwillingness to leave parents or perhaps a worldly fortune.

Those who sincerely search for Christ, do not seek in vain. Think of the many who have found Him as converts to the Catholic church. Many too have found Him again aften long years away from their religious duties. Others find him through following their vocation. What a marvelous privilege to attend Mass and receive Him in Holy Communion, yes, to truly find Him in our hearts and to appreciate more deeply the great honor bestowed upon His children. "You are the temple of the living God" (2 Cor. 6, 16).

Moreover, in this meditation, I have learned through the example of Christ the supreme importance of one thing, "My Father's business," or in other words, God's holy Will. This, in future, will be my one and only ambition, to fulfill the Will of my Father, taking as example, Christ the model Son. Conclude with an *Our Father*.

The Hidden Life

Here we come to a meditation that the world at large will never understand. It is given to only a few to appreciate and to love the hidden life. Occupation, as we shall see, is not a hindrance to the hidden life. It is an active life exteriorly, but with a very important interior motive which gives to each action of the day an eternal merit.

The scene:

Let us try to see the little house at Nazareth, and to be the guest of Jesus, Mary and Joseph. Listen to their conversation, observe their actions and courtesy as the best example of etiquette we could find (Luke 2, 51-52).

The petition:

Let us ask for the grace not only to appreciate the hidden life at Nazareth, but to make it the model of our own life.

THE HOME AT NAZARETH

After that first recorded word of her Son: "I must be about my Father's buiness," Mary may well have expected that she must be prepared to be often separated from her Son. She must not wish to keep Him in obscurity in such an out-of-the-way place as Nazareth when He might be doing "His Father's business," that is, teaching even the learned doctors in the great temple at Jerusalem. However, it was not with the doctors or the learned men, but strange to say, in that little cottage at Nazareth that His Father's business was to be carried on.

For eighteen years more, Jesus will be subject to His parents, and, while living in obscurity, will advance in wisdom and grace.

To love the cross is at all times to love to be hidden and unknown. "Love to be unknown," says the *Imitation of Christ,* and again: "No one is safe in coming forward who does not gladly remain in obscurity." Now I have come to Nazareth to learn how the "Father's business" can be done in obscurity and humility. Approaching the home what do I see and hear?

Mary welcomes me into her little home. What a privilege to be here. She seems to lead my attention to the nearby workshop. I begin to look around and notice the great pieces of wood, the rough tools, the odor of pinewood freshly cut, a few articles in the making.

It is quite evident that nothing very grand is done here. There is no fine or artistic work no signs of exceptional skill. There is simply the work that a village carpenter anywhere would have: a cartwheel to repair, a handle for a spade, a small table in the making. This is the setting; this is where Joseph the carpenter and Jesus the apprentice carry on their work.

THE CARPENTER

Although Mary has directed my attention to the little workshop and seems to take a personal interest in each unfinished piece of work lying about, my own thoughts are closer to her. I am standing alongside the mother of God. I feel that I should be on my knees instead of just standing there. My heart has been won forever by her simplicity. Mary. And then I notice her sudden glance to the doorway. Jesus and Joseph have returned from one of their customary errands, evidently they have just been delivering some piece of their work. In her sweet voice, Mary introduces me.

What is my first reaction to this meeting? Jesus, the boy Jesus? Yes, I had looked at Him before in the temple; then He seemed too far away. He was teaching. There was something too solemn about it all. But this is home, His home... and His eyes are looking right into mine. Dear God, I want to cast myself right at His feet. But I am stopped. Has He understood my embarrassment, my timidity or whatever it is? He has drawn me to Himself with an outstretched hand. And then I feel His hand, not so soft, but the hand of a worker. It is the hand of Jesus; and I feel that I can hold it forever.

After a short rest, work is resumed. Tools in hand, they begin, and right here I am taken completely by surprise. I hear Jesus asking St. Joseph's advice about something he is doing. He who created the world and whose hands have fashioned everything in it is asking advice from one of his creatures. How different from most of us who consider our way the best, and so often refrain from asking the advice of others. Nazareth ... humility!

"HE WAS SUBJECT TO THEM"

How much thought for meditation these few words give us. He was obedient. He does not thrust His own ideas on His parents, or try to make them see His point of view. He takes the place of an inferior, of a child. How important, then, He knew this example would be in our own lives, because He will give us the very same direction as He did to His apostles: "Unless you become as little children, you shall not enter into the kingdom of heaven."

In our meditation, let us focus our attention once more on the young boy, Jesus. He who is God, listens to Mary His mother and follows her advice. And on her part she was still living a beautiful life of faith. Mary had believed from the hour that Gabriel had spoken to her that God was really within her. Later, she believed that the little child whom she rocked to sleep was God, yes, that it was God whom she had taught to walk and to speak. And now she sees Him advance in age and wisdom and she feels her love advancing also. How wonderful it is to be the mother of God.

How long was He subject to Mary and Joseph? All those years at Nazareth. What beautiful lessons of humility, obedience and love do we see here at Nazareth ... the most perfect home in the world.

How wonderful the ways of God. Here at Nazareth we have seen nothing but the simplicity of home life, and yet Christ is accomplishing the salvation of mankind, no less than when He will die upon the cross.

At Nazareth He won for us the grace to sanctify the most ordinary duties of our daily life. Do I fully realize that the Morning Offering makes each one of my actions throughout the day meritorious for all eternity? There are so many routine actions of daily life—dressing in the morning, washing, preparing meals, cleaning, mending, gardening, shopping and other duties so familiar to a home. And all the while, God is present. He wants to receive our morning prayers, He wants to hear His blessing invoked at mealtime, and finally, at the end of the day, how He must love to join the family at Rosary time. Yes, our home can be another Nazareth. And what a blessing for us dear father, mother and family when it may also be said of our home as it was said of His: "No wonder that your home was ground the angels loved to tread."

Indeed the angels were continually looking upon the Holy Family at Nazareth. In the simple life of the poor they beheld their King and Queen. It was not the work at Nazareth that counted so much as the reason why it was being done namely to honor and serve God the Father. Only recently Pope Paul in speaking to a large group of workers told them: "Rediscovery of the real meaning of Christ is the answer to the problem of the working classes." And the real meaning of Christ is: Brotherhood. The Holy Father has spoken so clearly, "It is He who becoming our flesh, sanctifies and blesses the things of earth and of life and Who teaches us to discover in them wisdom and beauty." Nazareth teaches wisdom and beauty at its best. Christ was a worker. Today He alone understands completely the heart of the working man and woman. For all the security and peace that men are seeking—Nazareth has the answer. In concluding my little meditation, I will say a little prayer to Jesus, Mary and Joseph.

The Two Standards

Long ago we chose the Standard of Christ. We are animated with only one desire, namely to model our entire lives on that of our Leader. However, it is not sufficient to be enlisted in His army, to have sworn to follow Him, we must study His strategy, that we may more effectually fight with Him and like Him. We must also study the strategy of Satan that we may be aware of his traitorous snares. The eternal struggle between Christ and Satan, between good and evil, is the central point of history. Around Christ today there are millions of faithful souls in every path of life. Around Satan and his camp are those countless deluded souls who are trying to banish God and the idea of God from their fellowmen. Their principal aim is to pervert the minds and hearts of the young. Here St. Ignatius offers a meditation most practical for today.

The scene:

I shall try to visualize, "a vast plain embracing the whole region around Jerusalem, where stands the Supreme Captain of the faithful...Christ! And another plain in the region of Babylon, where the chief enemy Lucifer is found."

The petition:

I will ask for "knowledge of the deceits of the wicked chieftain, and for help to guard against them, and for knowledge of the true life which our Sovereign and true Leader points out, and for the grace to imitate Him." In other words: Seek the Divine Will and follow it.

THE STANDARD OF SATAN

Here I will endeavor to see the world divided and represented by two prominent cities, Jerusalem and Babylon. Peace reigns in the city of God; confusion in the city of Satan. One city is united in obedience; the other disunited in rebellion.

Now I shall study the standard of Lucifer, the mortal enemy of mankind. He is a fallen angel, with all the intelligence of an angel, but directed toward evil. I shall try to see the picture as St. Ignatius portrays him in that vast plain of Babylon, seated on a lofty throne of fire and smoke. What are the characteristic marks of Satan? His motive is hatred. He is dominated by a spirit of rebellion and criticism. He is jealous of his power and strives to conquer the souls of men through deceit, confusion, fear and terror. How terrible his ways, the flashing attractiveness of fire, the deceit and obscurity of smoke! These characteristics are seen today, the flashing and gaudy attractions of the hour that come and go like a wisp of smoke often leaving sin and sorrow in their wake. Satan is the master of deceit. His appeal is to satisfy the senses, the imagination and the passions of man. He is well informed in the art of transforming himself now in one way, now in another. If St. Ignatius were alive today he would certainly turn to the youth of our country and beg them "to ask for knowledge of the deceits of the wicked chieftain." Satan leads the communist camp.

Satan wants all souls to follow the path of sin. He makes various insidious suggestions to the young in order to get them started in the wrong direction. We can imagine him making suggestions such as these:

Why wait any longer? Do what you want to do now; your parents don't understand. Satan strikes at lawful obedience. Why not be like the others? They drink and enjoy life. Why don't you read the book? You are old enough to read anything. Why not tell a lie? It will certainly be embarassing if you don't cheat. Why everybody cheats.

Satan makes countless suggestions, which can and often do, lead to serious sin. Our aim must be to avoid all sin.

There is one fact in particular which I must bear in mind regarding the universal strategy of Satan. He can work only with *good things*. All the things which God has made are good. The devil makes nothing. He can only abuse, disfigure or misrepresent to the minds of people, objects which are good in themselves.

Since the advent of the Christian religion, the devil

models his false mysticism after the pattern of the true faith. A false worship must seem like Christianity. Consequently Satan uses very subtle means of obscuring the truth by spreading statements that *seem like* the truth: All religions are fundamentally the same. Why should there be any fixed type of religion? What is Satan aiming at constantly? He is aiming at confusion, rebellion, civil strife, unrest. What means does he use? He works with evil doers against the good. He works with the means of fear, hatred and pride. Satan is pushing hard to eliminate God and the image of God in the souls of men. He is urging youth in particular to laugh at immodesty, to laugh at sin. Day by day his tactics are becoming more open and deceitful. Knowing the ways of Satan and our own weakness, our Lord—Himself being tempted by Satan—has for each one of us this salutary advice: Watch and pray!

To avoid any snare of Satan, I will turn to God and ask for the grace, that is, knowledge of the wicked enemy of my soul.

THE UNIVERSAL ATTACK

In the *Spiritual Exercises,* this fact is made very clear. Satan summons together innumerable devils and disperses them to go, "some to one city, some to another, and so on throughout the whole world, omitting not any provinces, places, or states of life, or any persons in particular."

St. Paul in writing to the Ephesians (Chap. 6, 11-17) warns them and ourselves, "Put on the armor of God, that you may be able to stand against the deceits of the devil. For our wrestling is not against flesh and blood but against the Principalities and Powers, against the rulers of the world of darkness, against the spirits of wickedness in high places. Therefore take unto you the armor of God, that you may be able to resist in the evil day, and to stand in all things perfect. Stand therefore, having your loins girt about with truth, and having on the breastplate of justice, and your feet shod with the preparation of the Gospel of peace: In all things taking the shield of faith, wherewith you may be able to extinguish all the fiery darts of the most wicked one. And take unto you the helmet of salvation, and the word of the Spirit, which is the word of God." There is much matter here for serious thought and prayer.

In what does the universal attack of Satan consist? Briefly, the infernal strategy consists in tempting man by the allurement of richness. Wealth leads toward the desire for honor. Striving for wealth and honor, spiritual values are lost. Worldly ambition leads to pride. If a man is proud, he is merely a tool in the hand of Satan. Self has increased and God has decreased, and Satan is ready to propose one final step...deliberate mortal sin.

Satan's plan aims toward separation. He tries constantly to bring friend against friend, brother against brother, husband against wife. He aims at discord between families, internal strife in a nation and war between nations. Against this conflict of hatred which today is a very serious menace to world peace, we turn to our Blessed Lady who is the Queen of Peace.

THE STANDARD OF CHRIST

Now we turn our thoughts to the standard of Christ. Our true and supreme Captain, Christ the King, lovable in every respect, takes His stand on a lowly spot in a great plain near Jerusalem. How often the gentle Christ walked along the peaceful roadways of Judea surrounded by simple peasants. In my imagination I will try to picture Him going from village to village. How does he look? What does he say? What is the particular mission of our Lord? Above all, He is seeking for generous souls whom He may first call to Himself, instruct in His sacred doctrine, and then send them to preach His gospel of love. Yes, I realize He has been doing this since the time He called Peter, Andrew and the others. He told them, "Come after Me, and I will make you fishers of men" (Mark 1, 17).

The call of Christ is universal. Again I hear the voice of the Good Shepherd. "I know mine and mine know Me." There is no question about His knowing and loving each of His sheep intimately. But do the sheep know Him? So many do not. Do I listen to His voice urging me to make Him known? Do I hear and appreciate the voice of my Shepherd when He speaks to me through His Vicar upon earth? Recently Pope Paul expressed these thoughts: "Today the Will of Christ is pressing upon us and obliging us to do all that we can with love and wisdom to bring all Christians the supreme blessing and honor of a united Church." The Good Shepherd prayed that His Church would be one.

Do I realize that Christ is calling me *now* to do my share in His work?

The Standard of Christ is one of humility and love. He begs me to learn of Him. "Learn of Me, because I am meek and humble of heart." But how am I to attain Christ-like humility? There is only one way and that is to submit to humiliations through a love of Christ. Here

I realize that the constant enemy is *self*. It is so natural to seek and accept the praise of others and to resent correction. I must pray for the supernatural grace of humility and not lose sight of my goal. The cross is the Standard of Christ. I am pledged to His Standard, but do I follow Him with humility and generosity?

In the world of today, the contrast between the standard of Satan and that of Christ is so apparent. Satan is aiming at separation; Christ at unity. Satan wants my love to be directed toward material things that will perish; Christ bids me to seek first the kingdom of God, that will remain forever. I recognize the struggle within my soul and turn to Christ with renewed confidence in this meditation. What else matters if God is mine!

It is God's Holy Will that we live united to Him. Each of the sacraments carries the grace of union. In Baptism the soul is united with God for the first time. Confession unites the sinner with God. The Holy Eucharist sustains the union; Confirmation strengthens it. In the sacraments of Matrimony, the union of husband and wife is symbolic of Christ and His Church. Holy Orders unites the priest with God in the Sacred ministry. And lastly, Extreme Unction is the final purification of one's soul for eternal union with God. The Standard of Christ leads always to the eternal possession of God. Eternal union!

At the close of this meditation I shall speak first with our Blessed Mother, then with our Blessed Lord, and lastly with the Eternal Father begging for the grace to be delivered from the snares of Satan and to follow the Standard of Christ in my daily life.

The Public Life of Christ

Sooner or later one element enters into the life of all of us. It is separation. Young men and women leave home for one reason or another, perhaps to attend school, enter military service, or go on a foreign mission. It is never easy for a family to be separated from their loved ones. Fortunately, our Good Shepherd has given us an example that will bring strength and encouragement in our own hour of separation.

The scene:

> Picture Jesus leaving His happy home at Nazareth and then being baptized by St. John in the river Jordan (Luke 3, 21-23).

The petition:

> Here again I will ask for the grace to know Christ better in order that I may love Him the more deeply and imitate Him more closely.

JESUS LEAVES NAZARETH

Now that the years of His hidden life have come to a close and He is about to do His Father's business publicly, Jesus must leave the happiest little home upon earth. He must say goodbye to His mother. Had He been able to earn enough for her future support, or would she have to live on charity? We do not know. But this is certain regarding Himself: He had no fixed place of abode from this time on. "The foxes have holes and the birds of the air nests, but the Son of Man hath not where to lay His head" (Luke 9, 58). After He had gathered around Him His twelve apostles, how often the little band lacked food and shelter. Frequently the canopy of heaven was their only roof.

Jesus left Nazareth's warm home and the mother who had transformed the carpenter's house into the home of the Son of God. When the day of departure came, He asked this great sacrifice of Mary. She had to surrender Him because His Father's business was calling Him elsewhere. The world needed His message. We needed His example.

Mary's heart was breaking when she saw Him go. No one had ever known Jesus as she knew Him, and no one ever loved Him as she had. Their mutual love was the most perfect on earth. For thirty years He had been the life of her life. She was the only mother in the world who could worship her son as her God. Now she had to give Him up. She would not keep Him back from the work He was going to do, because she had learned from Him the value of souls. Parting with Him was worse than death itself. But she accepts it as the Holy Will of God.

And what were Mary's thoughts when Jesus went away? The Mother of Jesus stood in the doorway, gazing off into the distance. Her hands hung limp and quiet by her side. Her sweet face was partly uplifted. Her gaze was thinking of Him as a baby at Bethlehem. She saw again the sudden flight into Egypt, the return to Nazareth. She recalled Him as a young boy and remembered how she had been to find Him after the three days' search in Jerusalem. What was it He had said? She could never forget those words: "Did you not know that I must be about my Father's business?"

Her thoughts were still of Him. But her thoughts

were hers alone. No one shared them. No one but she, now that Joseph was dead, really knew her child for what He was. Jesus had left her, for her little boy had grown to manhood. In His kind manly and gentle way, He had bade her goodbye. His going made her think of His coming. Mary could look back to the day when Jesus had first come to her. It was her word that had made Him come. "Be it done unto me according to thy word." Those words had made her the mother of God.

Throughout that day of His departure, Mary kept her thoughts on Jesus. A hundred times she looked up startled as she fancied she heard His step. His shadow seemed to fall across the threshold. And now it was evening, quiet and peaceful evening. From the porch of her little cottage, Mary gazed out over the horizon. Then she began to feel Her comradeship with all the mothers of men. Her loneliness seemed to disappear. Once again her soul seemed to sing that beautiful *Magnificat*: "My soul doth magnify the Lord." In the last rays of the beautiful sunset, all the landscape seemed aglow with its crimson and gold. Mary rejoiced that other souls would come to magnify the Lord. She had given her Son to the world. Do I fully appreciate her sacrifice?

If Mary had written a book relating the events of her life up to the present, how wonderful it would be for us to turn to it and read *Mary's Book*. But God does not want us to go to a book. He wants us to go to Mary Herself. In the depths of her soul's peace and joy, she possesses God because of her motherhood. In the inner reality of her spiritual life, she is possessed by God. And because of Him, "all generations shall call me blessed." She feels her motherhood extending to all those whom her Son had come to save. Mother Mary, how ineffably much you have meant to souls, and to my soul. Please accept my heartfelt gratitude.

THE BAPTISM

From Nazareth, our Lord went straight down to the bank of the Jordan where John, His faithful precursor, was preaching that the Kingdom of Heaven was at hand, and was baptizing the people. John had been for some time preparing the way for the King in the hearts of the people of Judea by telling them of their sins and urging the necessity of doing penance for them. As a consequence they had flocked out to the desert of Perea on the other side of the Jordan to confess their sins and be baptized by him.

Although John was expecting Jesus to show Himself to the people, he was surprised to find Him presenting Himself for Baptism among the crowd of sinners. He did not at first recognize Jesus, but the coming of someone to be baptized who had no sins to confess opened John's eyes. In his quandary he whispered to Jesus: "I have need to be baptized by Thee, and comest Thou to me?" Christ had no need of John's baptism, it is true. But He is a King Who has come to call His subjects to help Him in the great battle against sin. He would begin by making Himself one of them. For this our Lord goes down into the water. He is baptized for our sake, not for any stain on His sinless soul.

Thus did Jesus begin His public life with a humiliation. He allowed Himself to pass as someone far less than He was, even to the extent of permitting others to regard Him as a sinner. This He did for me, to teach me to accept humiliation if I am ever to resemble Him.

Then came the testimony of heaven. "Jesus also being baptized and praying, heaven was opened and the Holy Spirit descended in a bodily shape as a dove upon Him; and a voice came from heaven: This is My beloved Son in whom I am well pleased" (Matt. 3, 17).

John saw the Spirit come down as a dove and remain upon Jesus. He knew that Jesus was the Son of God of Whose kingdom there would be no end. He could now point Him out to the people as the long-promised Messiah. The Father had spoken: "This is My beloved Son. In Thee I am well pleased." For the first time the Holy Trinity, One God in Three Persons, showed itself to men: The Father in the Voice from Heaven; the Son in the Sacred Human Nature; and the Holy Spirit in the form of a dove. His Father set His seal upon Him. He had chosen to make Himself as a sinner, but His Father had restored His reputation publicly: "Thou art My beloved Son" (Mark 1, 11).

Would I be pleasing to the Father? Would I win His approval and be His beloved child? Then let me make use of two means which will not fail to gain for me my wish.

The first and most effective means toward a closer union with God is prayer. Meditation places our entire soul before Him and brings to us a more intimate knowledge of God and of ourselves. Besides, there are habits of prayer most essential in daily life: the morning offering to start and the act of perfect contrition to end the day. Before the family retires, what could be more devotional than the family Rosary? It is a beautiful step toward the receiving of Holy Communion by all of the family together.

Would you be more pleasing to the Father? Prayer

and the Sacraments are the most certain means. The
Sacrament of Penance in the life of a Catholic is like
the stem to the flower. When this Sacrament is received,
the soul is strengthened in the avoidance of sin and of
the occasions of sin. But the stem depends upon the
root. And in the life of one's soul, the root must be deep
and strong in the virtue predominant in this scene of
our Lord's life: the humility of Jesus and that of John
the Baptist who said, "He must increase, I must decrease."

At this time, I place myself in spirit as a sheep near
to the Good Shepherd. I ask Him for the grace to learn
something of the wisdom of God's own Son when He
said, "Learn of Me because I am meek and humble of
heart." Make my poor heart like unto Thine! Guide me
always in the spirit of this Psalm:

> The Lord is my shepherd; I shall
> not want.
> He maketh me to lie down in green
> pastures: he leadeth me beside
> the still waters.
> He restoreth my soul: he leadeth
> me in the paths of righteousness
> for his name's sake.
> Yea, though I walk through the
> valley of the shadow of death, I will
> fear no evil: for thou art with me; thy
> rod and thy staff they comfort me.
> Thou preparest a table before me in
> the presence of mine enemies: thou
> anointest my head with oil; my
> cup runneth over.
> Surely goodness and mercy shall

follow me all the days of my life:
and I will dwell in the house of
the Lord for ever.   psalm 23

The Marriage at Cana

A marriage took place centuries ago in an unimportant town in Palestine. Like countless others it would have been entirely forgotten were it not for one memorable circumstance: our Lord and His mother were present. Since this wedding at Cana, Christ has been present at thousands of marriages the world over, with His blessing and His grace, that is, for those who understand and appreciate this sacrament of mutual love and sacrifice.

The scene:

To witness the persons, the conversation and the miracle (John 2, 1-11).

The petition:

Ask our Lord for a better knowledge and appreciation of the sacrament of matrimony.

"JESUS WAS INVITED"

The young couple of Cana had Christ in mind before their marriage, although they had no idea how much His presence would mean on the day itself. Today, when young couples have Christ in mind before marriage, they are taking very important steps together especially toward the communion rail. These words spoken very gratefully could never be forgotten: "My wife and I made a retreat just before we were married." And as a result of this preparation "Jesus was invited" into their hearts on the wedding day itself. Such has been the prelude to many happy marriages celebrated at the altar with the blessing of a nuptial Mass. Here is the goal for Catholic couples.

But what does our youth of today learn about marriage? This is a question for our teachers and parents to answer conscientiously. This first question deals with courtship. Does this period fail to imply respect, courtesy and modesty? Where do I stand in this regard? Let us be honest with ourselves and with others. Courtship leading to marriage should be a happy period of life, and will be if I am willing to turn toward the One who will help the most to make and keep my marriage a happy one...as He did at Cana.

THE MIRACLE OF CANA

Here I should try to witness a scene that portrays so vividly the thoughtfulness and kindness in the hearts of Jesus and Mary. She was alert to foresee the host's embarrassment if the wine should fail. It did. And the wine failing, the mother of Jesus said to Him: "They have no wine." And Jesus answered: "Woman, what is that to me and to thee? My hour is not yet come." The word "woman" in Aramaic has the meaning of special reverence. Christ's answer were words of refusal and another lady might have said: "Well I guess that's that." But not Mary. Although the time for performing His miracles had not come, nevertheless another important feature of life had come, namely the power of Mary's intercession with her divine Son. The rest is known to all. Water was changed into wine at the bidding of

Christ and it was the very best. Consequently His presence at this marriage made it far happier than could have been anticipated. It was happier too because of Mary.

In the world today there is a great need for happy marriages, not merely on the wedding day but through the years that follow. In order that prospective marriages may be properly contracted and actual marriages sustained, there is often need for instructions, helpful advice and prayer. For these reasons, it seems fitting to add these considerations to the meditation. God wills that marriages be for His glory.

HIS GLORY

We are told by St. John that, "this the first of his miracles Jesus worked in Cana of Galilee; and he manifested his glory, and his disciples believed in him" (John 2, 11).

Marriages are intended to manifest God's glory. The sacramental aspect of marriage is twofold; the Creator is glorified, the union of husband and wife is sanctified. And the marriage is sustained through the mutual cooperation with God's grace.

In this meditation, understanding as I should the meaning and obligations of marriage, I should go a step further by considering the practical problems of daily life. The majority of marriage failures can be traced to selfishness. It is self that wounds or kills mutual love. Love means everything. The words of a certain young man on the completion of his retreat are worth quoting: "The retreat has meant this to me: I now love my wife more than ever before." Evidently this young man made his marriage the most important subject of his prayer.

He expresses something very important, an increase of love. An increase of love for one another leads to an increase of love for God.

Husband and wife bring glory to God through their creative act of begetting children. The birth of a child is always one of the most important things in the world. To frustrate the marriage act by preventing conception is a mortal sin. Furthermore, to destroy the unborn child is one of the most serious of all crimes for this act not only kills the body but deprives the soul of baptism and consequently the beatific vision of God. On the contrary, parents who have cooperated with God in helping souls to attain this vision of the blessed are rendering the greatest possible glory to Him.

How consoling it has been to witness the kindness of our Blessed Lord and His mother. This marriage feast at Cana is one of the treasured incidents in the public life of Jesus. That He should not disdain to be a Guest at this wedding feast certainly adds a revealing touch to the portrait of the God-Man that we cannot afford to miss. He desires our human and spiritual joy to ever increase. "Again, I say to you rejoice!"

Mary's heart has not changed. We are bid to ask her intercession for the welfare of our body and soul. She desires that our norm of life be according to God's Holy Will. If I were so privileged to hear her voice—what would my mother advise? "Do whatever He tells you." Her words at Cana are now addressed to me. Dear mother, I am thankful to you.

In concluding my meditation, I should thank God for my good parents. As at Cana what blessings come today when marriages are blest by Christ. I will ask His grace to realize more deeply the beauty of a happy union on earth that leads to an eternal union of happiness in heaven, with Jesus my King, and Mary my Queen!

The Sermon on the Mount

During the public life of our Lord, He preached in many places and to all classes of people. On one particular occasion after speaking to the multitudes we read, "the people were in admiration at his doctrine for he was teaching them as one having power and not as the Scribes and Pharisees" (Matt. 7, 28-29). Many from that time to the present have also been in admiration of Christ's beautiful and inspiring sermon on the mount.

The scene:

> To picture myself as a witness to this sermon (Matt. 7).

The petition:

> I will ask for the grace to understand and appreciate more deeply the wisdom of Christ's doctrine.

THE BEATITUDES

Often we are more favorably impressed by deeds rather than words. In the sermon on the Mount we are impressed by both. It may be interesting to note that the sermon was given between miraculous deeds of charity. Just prior to this sermon we read, "and they presented to him all sick people ... and he cured them"

(Matt. 4, 24). Immediately following the sermon He cured a leper and the centurion's servant. Is it any wonder that the multitudes followed Him?

With the disciples, I, too, take my place at the feet of the Master, pressing as close as I may, so as not to miss a single word, glance or gesture. For "never did man speak as this Man." And all the while I diligently ponder every word and phrase of the heavenly wisdom here proposed. How different from the worldly minded! During this sermon I am not listening to one of the world's renowned philosophers, but to Eternal Wisdom speaking with human lips.

In the meditation on the Kingdom of Christ we learned of His campaign to conquer souls for the Kingdom of heaven. Although heaven is a gift it is also a reward. It must be won. Now from our Lord's sermon on the mount, we are not left in doubt regarding those who shall be eternally rewarded for keeping His laws.

It is clear from our Lord's words who the blessed really are. "Blessed are the poor in spirit...the meek... they that mourn...they that hunger and thirst after justice ...the merciful...the clean of heart...the peacemakers ...they that suffer persecution."

Here is the simple blueprint for happiness here and hereafter. But what was the result of this sermon? The Jews admired the wisdom of the beatitudes as well as other parts of His sermon, the multitudes followed Him. Today many admire His doctrine, but how many are willing to live His doctrine? It is simple enough to point to those who are not, but if I point to myself, what is the answer? What foolishness to choose vice instead of viritue. Briefly the good and evil are as follows:

Poor in spirit	. . . .	attachment to worldly goods.
Meekness	. . . .	sinful anger.
Mourn	. . . .	those who seek happiness in worldly pleasures.
Seekers of justice	. . . .	seekers of self.
Merciful toward others	. . . .	unmerciful and self indulgent.
Clean of heart	. . . .	impure in thought, word, and deed.
Peacemakers	. . . .	troublemakers.
Suffer persecution	. . . .	unwillingness to suffer persecution.

THE LIGHT OF THE WORLD

Immediately following the discourse on the Beatitudes, our Lord looks at His disciples and, able to penetrate the goodness of their hearts, speaks words of encouragement: "You are the salt of the earth." And then He goes on to tell them, "You are the light of the world" (Matt 5, 13, 14).

There is a marked contrast between the two images as also between the comments which our Lord makes upon each. The disciples are first the salt of the earth and then the light of the world. Salt is very necessary for the seasoning and preservation of food. It is a very common and useful creature. Light is essential also, and one of the most beautiful works of God. By way of similitude, our Lord speaks of these elements of salt and light to express His higher meaning in the supernatural order.

The disciples called by God to a supernatural life through Baptism, have the duty of preserving the world from corruption and giving a good flavor to life by means of their personal influence on society. What a wonderful vocation! "You are the light of the world," which signifies that you have been blest by God to become an instrument for His greater glory. "So let your light shine before men, that they may see your good works, and glorify your Father who is in heaven."

What our Lord said to His disciples, He says to me. Good works are not to be done for the sake of worldly honor and applause but to manifest God's law to others by word and example. "You are the light of the world. A city that is set on a hill cannot be hid." A soul that is built firmly on prayer and humility cannot be hidden. There is so much good to be done today through good example and the willingness to teach others. Think what it means to bring one soul to Christ! A few souls! A dear old German priest expressed the thought in these words, "If we cannot be all things to all men, like St. Paul... at least we can be a little to a few."

When our Lord addresses me with these words of encouragement and obligation to help others...."You are the light of the world," what is my personal reaction?

OTHER CHRISTS

The Sermon on the Mount had a very definite purpose especially for our Lord's own chosen apostles. Their lives were to be a fulfillment of the law of charity. They were to be teachers of Christ's doctrine by word and example. Briefly: they were to be other Christs. With the exception of Judas they did become other Christs. We celebrate their feast days; we honor them for what they were and for what they did for God. But often we forget our own personal calling...to be another Christ! What is it that will help most of all? It is *kindness* that makes life worth living as Jesus taught and lived it.

For a Christian to follow in the footsteps of Christ means that super human strength is needed. The only strength of soul lies in its union with God; weakness of soul consists only in its separation from Him. This necessary strength, this solid foundation of soul Christ speaks of when concluding His sermon on the Mount. After giving a perfect explanation of His doctrine, He speaks as follows, "Every one therefore that heareth these my words, and doth them, shall be likened to a wise man that built his house upon a rock: And the rain fell, and the floods came, and the winds blew, and they beat upon that house, and it fell not, for it was founded on a rock."

Our Lord tells us that it is as dangerous to hear and not to keep His words, as it is to preach them and not to practice them. "And every one that heareth these my words, and doth them not, shall be like a foolish man that built his house upon the sand: And the rain fell, and floods came, and the winds blew, and they beat upon that house, and it fell, and great was the fall thereof" (Matt. 7, 24-27).

From the passages just quoted, our Lord seems to forewarn His followers that all kinds of trial will test the strength of their souls. How important that He be near us at all times.

Christ desires that we hear His words and keep them. In this way our spiritual life will not be undermined by the trials and temptations of life, but will be strong in Him, and by Him and for Him. This is to be...another Christ!

In my prayer now I will turn to our Blessed Lord

and ask for the grace to know and to fulfill His Holy Will. Whatever He has promised as a reward for fidelity, He promises today and to me, because He has not changed nor ever will, "Jesus Christ, yesterday, and today, and the same forever" (Heb. 13, 8).

Christ is my changeless Friend. Only in God can any human heart be satisfied. I will take to heart the beautiful —and oh, so true!—words of St. Augustine: "Thou hast made me for Thyself, O God, and my heart can find no rest until it rest in Thee." Now at the feet of my Good Shepherd, I will speak to Him, listen to His message and realize that He is calling me to the life of His Blessed.

Christ with His Apostles

In this meditation we are brought to realize that each one of us can be an apostle in his or her own sphere of life. Our Lord loved His apostles dearly, but they needed every bit of His teaching before they could be other shepherds. If I am going to be another apostle, I must learn from the Good Shepherd how He wants me to be His instrument for good. Our faith is spread by good example at school, at home, and in our place of occupation.

The scene:

See our Lord in prayer on the mountainside; witness His coming to the apostles on the water. (Matt. 15, 13-34).

The petition:

Ask the grace of sustained confidence in God.

THE ZEAL AND PRAYER OF CHRIST

It was during the second year of His ministry that Christ called Peter and Andrew, James and John, Philip and Nathaniel. He had worked many miracles, preached many sermons and was well known all over Galilee. The apostles had followed Him, listened to Him and had been sent on their first mission tour "through the towns, preaching and healing everywhere." The news of John the Baptist's murder had just arrived. "When Jesus heard of it, He took His disciples and went into a desert place apart." But a great multitude followed Him and "He had compassion on them and healed their sick." In the evening the apostles wanted Him to dismiss the multitude, but His thoughtfulness and kindness would not permit this. He fed the five thousand by the multiplication of the loaves and fishes. Such was the Master's zeal; it was an entire giving of Himself to the work He had come to do. And after dismissing the multitude He went into the mountain alone to pray. And what command did He give the apostles when they were content to remain right where they were? "Go to the opposite shore." An order of obedience came just when they least expected it, and an order which would mean a separation from their Master. The apostles obey, and our Lord is left alone to pray. Not that He needed to pray, but we needed His example. If we are to be about "our Father's business" we must have frequent recourse to Him, asking for grace and strength and light to know His will and to follow it. I will listen to the voice of my Shepherd "Take my hand.... I understand."

THE APOSTLES ALONE

They had spent a long day in the society of their Master, and now they are alone. They are tired after nine hours of rowing. Jesus is not with them. A storm begins to toss the little boat to and fro. Now the apostles are in desolation. They had seen Him multiplying the loaves, yet now, in their trouble, they do not turn to Him. How like ourselves.

At about four in the morning when they were three or four miles from the shore, they saw someone walking on the sea. Terrified, they cried out for fear. But immediately Jesus spoke to them saying: "Be of good heart. It is I, fear ye not."

He had seen them all the time. They were not really alone; He had watched all their efforts and was ready to come at the right moment. It was like them, and like us too, not to recognize Him, not to see at first that which seems like another difficulty is really Jesus in disguise. "Fear not, it is I." What they feared so much proved to be their greatest help. Let me remember this when my own difficulties arise: Jesus is always present.

PETER IS BID TO COME TO JESUS

"And Peter, making answer said: Lord, if it be Thou, bid me to come to Thee upon the waters." And He said: "Come." And Peter going down out of the boat, walked upon the water to come to Jesus. Peter had no doubt about the apparition being His Master. His request to be allowed to go to Him was not a test as to whether or not it really was the Master, it was simply the desire of his impetuous, loving heart to be with His Master.

He knew that he could not walk on the water, but he also knew that his Master could give him the power to do it, so he said: "Bid me come to Thee upon the waters." Perhaps my last retreat resolution looks impossible for me, but the answer of the Master is: *Come.* Step down fearlessly into the waters; do what seems impossible, the responsibility is mine. Abandon yourself entirely into My hands.

"Come." The word is enough for Peter, for he loved his Master. "And going down out of the boat he walked upon the water to go to Jesus." What a wonderful sight for the other apostles. But suddenly they saw him sinking beneath the waves. What had happened? Seeing the wind strong, he was afraid, and when he began to sink, he cried out: "Lord, save me." Was not the wind strong before?" What had changed? Peter's confidence, that is all. The circumstances were exactly the same as when he walked so courageously on the water a minute before; the wind, the waves and the darkness. What had made him lose his trust? *Seeing* the waves. He began to look at them. He had taken his eyes off the Master to look at the difficulties; a fatal thing to do. Perhaps a little vanity; when he saw how well he was getting on and that it was not nearly so difficult as he had expected. Perhaps he even looked around to make sure that his companions were watching him. We do not know. But for ourselves, how prone we are when we are doing well to be proud of it, to hope that others are noticing it. Satan is very busy at such times, because he is more likely to catch us off our guard in time of success than in time of failure. Peter lost his confidence and began to sink. But he did the best thing possible; he cried out to the Master for help: "Lord save me." And immediately Jesus stretching forth

His hand took hold of him and said to him: "O thou of little faith, why didst thou doubt?" He led him back to the boat. Peter did not feel now that he had anything to be proud of before the others.

What is the lesson for ourselves? It is not sufficient to make one big act of confidence during our retreat; that confidence has to be sustained amid all the winds and waves that trouble the surface of life's sea. There is only one way of doing it, and that is to keep up the intimacy of the retreat, to live always in the presence of Jesus. And when by the weakness of our human nature we begin to sink, let Him be our first thought: Lord save me. Those who act thus will find themselves walking hand in hand with Jesus through the difficulties. We must learn that *all* is His doing, the storm and the calm...both are intended to lead us to Him.

We have resolved to serve the Divine Master. We decide to succeed in some work undertaken for Him... and He comes to us in failure and humiliation. We had hoped to find Him in laboring for Him...and He comes to us in sickness. We had hoped to find Him in more fervor and He comes to us in aridity and desolation. And we fail to recognize him.

Yes, I have failed so often. But I shall take hope from the words of St. Paul: "I can do all things in Him who strengthens me." So now I place myself more completely in the hands of the Good Shepherd, and speak to Him: Dear Jesus, be my strength now and in the future—please. Let me ever be mindful of my weakness and inability to make any progress at all without Your help. Let each morning find me looking up with confidence that You have given me this day and this hour for a definite purpose.

Let Your own words be in my heart, "I come to do Thy will, O God." Let me express them in the prayer You spoke for the first time in uniting my soul with God: "Our Father, Who art in heaven...".

Christ's Visit to Bethany

Sincere friendship is a real blessing. Throughout the Gospel narrative, whether in the company of little children, the doctors in the temple, the farmers, the fishermen, or the outcasts of society, our Lord was always a true friend to all.

In this meditation, I shall see Him visiting His friends in Bethany, a city only a few miles from Jerusalem. The circumstances of this particular visit make it one of the most memorable of His Life. Lazarus had very recently died and was buried. Mary sat at home weeping, surrounded by loving friends who sought in vain to console her. Martha, having heard that Jesus was approaching Bethany, went immediately to meet Him.

The scene:

Here we picture the little home of Martha and Mary. We see our Lord with them. We listen to their conversation in order to appreciate more fully their true Friend and mine (St. John 11).

The petition:

To ask for the grace to profit from the message of Christ to His friends: "One thing is necessary," Love.

MARTHA

This is St. John's description (Chap. 11). "Martha therefore as soon as she heard that Jesus was come, went to meet Him, but Mary sat at home." Martha had not a moment to lose. One more glance at the oven, a few pieces of kindling tossed on the fire, and final stir of the pot, and she was gone, down the path, and out the gate.

Near the city she met our Lord, and being unable to withhold from Him one moment longer the thought uppermost in her mind, she said, "Lord, if Thou hadst been here, my brother would not have died." She caught the pity in His eyes, and then continued, "But now also I know that whatsoever Thou wilt ask of God, God will give it to Thee." There was more than human pity in His eyes.

In one of the most beautiful passages in Holy Scripture, "Jesus said to her: 'thy brother shall rise again.' Martha replied: 'I know that he shall rise again in the resurrection at the last day.' Jesus said to her, 'I am the resurrection and the life: he that believeth in me, although he be dead, shall live: And everyone that liveth and believeth in me shall not die forever. Believest thou this?' She said to Him, 'Yea, Lord, I believe that thou art the Christ the Son of the living God, who art come into this world.'" This was her perfect act of faith, and it is mine also.

MARY

Martha, realizing how much this visit of our Lord would mean to her sister, hurried directly to Mary to break the good news. "The Master is here and calleth for thee."

How these words touched the heart of Mary! Her personal friend was near, the One Who had forgiven her and raised her to a new and pure life. If He knew that her brother was sick and dying, why had he not come sooner?

Mary hurried to the feet of our Lord, and scarcely able to hold back her tears of grief, said to Him, "Lord, if thou hadst been here my brother would not have died." These were the same words that Martha spoke. Could our Lord have prevented their sorrow? Certainly. But He permitted it for a definite purpose. God always acts for the best. On this occasion He chose to elevate the souls of Mary and Martha to a higher life.

On a former visit to these same friends He had said, "One thing alone is necessary." He had implied that this was Love. Now He was proving the truth of His statement. Divine Love overshadows sorrow and death. Our Lord spoke divinely when He said "I am the resurrection and the life." He could, being Divine, restore and save natural life. But He had come into the world for something far greater—to restore and save supernatural life. This He did in Mary's soul.

Christ looks into the future and beholds another scene. Mary is again at His feet, as she had often been before. But now the sacred feet are nailed to a cross. Mary is kneeling at the foot of the cross. Above her, His Sacred Heart is calling to her with infinite love. "The Master is here and calleth for thee." Yes, on the cross He was calling for a return of love, and Mary is giving Him her love to the end.

This is the same Jesus who is calling for my love

now. What is my response? Do I love to attend Him at Holy Mass? Do I look at the little tabernacle with eyes of faith? Indeed, it is still true, "The Master is here and calleth for thee."

As at Bethany, He journeys the long distance to be with me, asking only that I take the few steps to His Presence. And when I come and possess Christ in my soul, I possess "the resurrection and the life." What greater joy could I desire on earth? "Believest thou this?" Lord, I believe. I pray I shall never lose this tremendous gift of faith. I shall esteem it above all else. And finally, after a life of faith, when Christ comes at death, He will be my Friend. "The Master is here and calleth for thee." Through the door of death I shall hurry to Him Who is resurrection and eternal life.

LAZARUS

Continuing in my meditation on the words of St. John who relates this event, I find one short sentence most expressive. It describes our Lord upon His arrival at the tomb of Lazarus: "And Jesus wept." The Jews who were present exclaimed aloud, "Behold how He loved him." In their lack of vision, they imagined that death was the end of love, the end of all. But the love of Christ overcomes even death itself.

Among the crowd were believers and unbelievers. Christ loved them all. He wanted all to believe in Him, even the weakest. For the strengthening of their faith, our Lord began a prayer that reveals the deep love of His Heart:

"Father, I give thee thanks that Thou hast heard me. And I know that Thou hearest me always; but because of the people who stand about me have I said it, that they may believe that Thou hast sent me."

In a tense, dramatic move, our Lord turned toward the tomb of Lazarus. All eyes were fixed on the door of the sepulchre. Our Lord lifted His voice in a piercing command: "Lazarus, come forth!" He who was the resurrection ordered the dead to arise. A miracle takes place in a strange impressive way. "And presently he that had been dead came forth, bound feet and hands." Our Lord then gave a short command to those standing by. "Loose him and let him go. Mary and Martha spring forward to unwind the cloths with which they had bound their brother. They, in this fear-filled but joyful service, complete the liberation of their dear one from death and the tomb.

Like Mary and Martha, I too can help in the liberation of countless souls, dead in sin bound by their evil ways. God wants to restore them in life. He wants my little prayers and daily sacrifices as part of His great work, the salvation of immortal souls. What will my answer be?

GOD'S PERSONAL CALL

From the very beginning God has called souls personally. "And the Lord called Adam and said to him, 'Where art thou?' And he said, 'I heard Thy voice in the garden and I was afraid.'" Then God called him to a life of penance.

Christ called Peter and the other apostles. We have seen their response to His Will. Christ called at least one rich young man who failed to respond. He called Zachaeus from a sycamore tree. Completely surprised the little Jew came quickly down to earth. People on the wayside aroused a poor blind man, "...Arise, He calleth thee!" And we are told that Bartimeus "leaped up and came to Him." He had reason to, as did Mary Magdalene.

Down through the ages men and women have received a personal call from our Lord. Today He hasn't ceased calling, but the trouble is that too many have been deaf to His call. Am I one of these? Do I make selfish excuses when I know that God is calling for a sacrifice that costs something?

To supply for the shortage of priests in the world, and especially in mission lands, surely God is calling young men into His sacred service. He is calling young women to the Sisterhood, and others to His lay apostolate. May souls today be alert to the call of the Master while there is yet time.

St. Paul spoke very clearly: "This is the Will of God, your sanctification." God's personal call to sanctity may come in any number of ways and perhaps at a time when least expected. St. Paul himself never expected to be knocked off his horse. God's call may come rather indirectly from witnessing the good example of someone else. His call may come during the time of retreat when a person is more than usually alert to His grace. But His voice requires that the soul be not only alert, but generous.

What better way to conclude this little meditation than by turning to our Lord and sincerely saying to Him:

"Dearest Lord, teach me to be generous. Teach me to serve Thee as Thou deservest; to give and not to count the cost; to fight and not to heed the wounds; to toil and not to seek for rest; to labor and not to seek reward, save that of knowing that I do Thy Will, O God. Amen."

The Three Degrees of Humility

Humility, being the foundation of all other virtues, is most worthy of my consideration and prayer. Christ ever appeals to humble souls and desires to lead them step by step. It may seem beyond my power to aspire to the third degree of humility, but Christ was speaking to all when He said: "Be perfect as your heavenly Father is perfect." Consequently, to every class of people and in every path of life, God's grace is present to assist each soul toward the highest perfection. If individuals fail it is not because His help was lacking; the fault is our own in failing to correspond with divine grace. We need humility and Christ is the example in word and deed. "Learn of Me, because I am meek and humble of heart."

The scene:

> To witness our Lord speaking to a mixed group of people together with His apostles, teaching them all the way to heaven through humility: "Unless you become as little children, you shall not enter the kingdom of heaven."

The petition:

> Ask the grace to be truly humble of heart, realizing that God is the source of all good.

THE FIRST DEGREE OF HUMILITY

St. Augustine clearly pointed out the difference between pride and humility when he said: "Pride is the love of self even to the contempt of God; humility is the love of God even to the contempt of self." From this we can infer that no one can be humble without a certain amount of contempt for self. There are various degrees, measured by the amount of love one has for God.

The first degree is absolutely necessary for salvation. One's contempt of self must be such that under no condition would a person deliberately offend God by committing mortal sin. The first degree consists, therefore, in the habitual disposition to obey God's law in all things.

Temptation comes. I must remember my own weakness and call upon God for help immediately. Why? Because so many far greater than I have fallen. The angels fell in heaven; our first parents in paradise; David, a man dear to the heart of God fell; so did Solomon, and Peter, so dear to the heart of Christ, although he had earnestly vowed: "Though I should died with Thee, I will not deny Thee." Peter's fault, lack of humility, may well be a lesson to me. A good confession is always a means of remaining in this first degree of humility.

THE SECOND DEGREE OF HUMILITY

Those who have attained this second degree must have such a contempt of self and such a love of God that they would rather die than commit a deliberate venial sin. In other words, I would not tell a deliberate lie to gain wealth, honor or even to save my life.

"The second degree is more perfect humility than the first; it consists in finding myself in such a state as not to desire nor to be more affected to have riches than poverty, to wish for honor than dishonor, to desire a long life than a short life, when the service of God, our Lord and the salvation of my soul are equal; and by this means never to enter into deliberation about committing a venial sin, neither for the sake of all created things, nor even if on that account men should deprive me of life."

The apostles before Pentecost belonged to this group. They would not think of sinning venially, but they still dreamed of the temporal kingdom with its earthly honor and glory. Nor were they prepared to suffer injuries and death for their King and Savior.

THE THIRD DEGREE OF HUMILITY

St. Ignatius speaks as follows: "The third degree is the most perfect humility; when, the first and second degree being included, and supposing equal praise and glory to the Divine Majesty, the better to imitate Christ our Lord and to become actually more like to Him, I desire and choose rather poverty with Christ poor, than riches; contempt with Christ condemned, than honors; and I desire to be esteemed as useless and foolish for Christ's sake, Who was first held to be such, than to be accounted wise and prudent in this world."

This may sound impossible. After Pentecost the apostles enjoyed this degree of humility. All through their lives they followed in the footsteps of Christ. This degree is associated with the meditation on the Kingdom of Christ. What does it mean in our everyday life?

It means that I shall not stand up for my rights. I could claim them; I could clear my reputation, but I will not because Christ did not. Sometimes I am tired, forgotten, left out, suffering, but I will not complain, but rather rejoice that I am like my Master again. I am free to choose between two courses in which I can glorify

God equally; I choose the less agreeable, the less attractive, because He would have done so.

Only those who love and want to love still more can belong to this degree. The Little Flower is a perfect example. And there are many today in every walk of life. A selfish person will never reach this degree; it belongs to those who are sincerely trying to become saints.

Granted that I try to avoid all sin, and occasions of sin; then I should try to practice this third degree of humility. How should I go about it? Calmly and prayerfully. I must understand that this is exactly what God wants of me. "This is the will of God, your sanctification." With this conviction in mind, then, I must be willing to take the means to learn more and more about my Good Shepherd. This means that I should arrange my life with time for prayer and meditation. Christ is the Teacher; His life is my daily lesson. The more I understand His life, the greater will be my appreciation. What did He choose? He chose a stable instead of a palace to be born. He chose poor parents. He could have enjoyed the best of everything but He chose the poorest. He could have had money, but He didn't carry a single coin. He borrowed one to point to the image of Caesar.

What did He do? He accomplished many wonderful things we read about in the New Testament. But these are not all. St. John concludes His gospel with the words: "There are also many other things which Jesus did...." Think of the good He did with His hands... a word from His lips and the sick were healed, the dead arose. Peter was converted by a glance of His eyes. And what of the many things that we don't know about? They were hidden from the eyes of the world, but not from His Father. Much of the public life of Christ remained hidden. And today He remains hidden in the hearts of those who love Him, especially the hearts of little children.

In the face of persecution, it has been the little ones in China who have been the most faithful. By nature timid and afraid, but with Christ strong and heroic. Themselves willing to suffer and die, that Christ may live. And this is in a similar way, the meaning of the third degree of humility: death to self that Christ may reign. St. Paul expresses the ideal: "And I live now not I, but Christ liveth in me."

In my prayer, I will turn to our Blessed Mother, to ask her intercession for the grace I need. Then I will renew my fidelity to Christ and through Him make my appeal to God with the prayer taught us by Christ, the "Our Father."

The Three Classes of Men

This meditation is in preparation for the Election or Reform of life. Whether this consideration of the Three Classes of Men is made during a retreat or outside of retreat—it is an uncompromising test of the sincerity of one's dispositions in regard to the service of God. In the meditation on the Two Standards it was definitely to Christ's standard that I pledged my fidelity. But a soldier of Christ must be tested. Do I have any inordinate affection toward some creature or creatures that would tend to separate me from the love which I owe to my Creator? My will must be tested. Furthermore, this test is made with God's help. Left to myself I shall fail. Therefore, I must understand clearly that although my part is important, God's part is absolutely necessary—"For it is God who worketh in you, both to will and to accomplish" (Phil. 11, 13).

The subject matter of this meditation is taken from an example of temporal wealth. St. Ignatius states the facts: "Three classes of men, each of which has acquired ten thousand ducats, not purely and duly for the love of God. They all desire to save their souls, to find in peace God our Lord, ridding themselves of the burden and impediment to this end which they find in their affection to the money acquired."

The scene:

> "It will be here to see myself standing before God our Lord and all His saints, that I may desire and know that which is more pleasing to His Divine Goodness."

The petition:

> "It will be here to beg the grace to choose that which is most for the glory of His Divine Majesty, and for the salvation of my soul."

THE FIRST CLASS

This first class represents men who wish to rid themselves of the inordinate affection for money that troubles their peace of mind. But do they *will* what they *desire?* What a contradiction! They look forward to the end but fail to take the means. Such is the case of a sick man who wants to be healed but refuses to see a doctor. Or again, it is the case of a person who wants to avoid mortal sin, but without avoiding the occasions.

One time our Lord invited a rich young man to be His follower. The young man had led a good life. Regarding the commandments he could honestly say, "All these I have kept from my youth, what is yet wanting to me?" (Luke 18-21).

"Jesus said to him, 'If thou will be perfect go and sell what thou hast and give to the poor... and come follow Me.'" In this case it is perfectly clear that worldly possessions would be a hindrance to the work of a true disciple.

"And when the young man heard this word, he went away sad, for he had great possessions." Here was a young man who came face to face with Christ; one whom we most likely would honor as a saint today had he followed the direction of the Master. But with his inordinate affection to worldly goods, he missed the greatest opportunity that Christ would offer. Now in my meditation, looking into my own soul, is there any obstacle keeping me away from God's service? Is my predominant passion one that I am willing to struggle against continually? And if actually called into His most intimate service, that of the religious life, would I also turn away sad?

THE SECOND CLASS

St. Ignatius describes this group very clearly when he writes: "The second class desire to shake off the affection, but they wish to shake it off in such a way as to remain in possession of what they have gained, so that God must come to what they desire: and they do not determine to leave the money in order to go to God, even though this would be the best state for them."

This class has some good will to conquer their inordinate affection, but not entirely. Such are like the sick man who is willing to take medicine of his own choice rather than what the doctor has prescribed as vitally necessary. Or again, like the individual who wants to avoid mortal sin, but continues to commit deliberate venial sins. There can be no compromise with sin. Pilate made Christ suffer more by his scheme of compromise. If there is reason to despise the attitude of Pilate—what about my own habitual reservations? I want to be a good Catholic, but with moderation: everyone cannot be a saint. I want to be charitable, but certain people don't suit my temperament, so I continue to avoid them as much as possible. Obedient! Yes, of course—but I like to do things my own way at least some times.

What does God think of this particular class of souls? Christ spoke very clearly regarding the spirit of compromise: "You cannot serve God and mammon" (Matt. 6, 24).

Moreover, anyone who tries to put his hand to the plough and looks back is never happy. God's blessing is not upon his work, not because of human frailty or mistakes, but because of following a standard less than God's own commandment to love Him..."with thy whole heart, thy whole soul, thy whole mind, and with thy whole strength."

THE THIRD CLASS

This group is described by St. Ignatius as follows: "The third class wish to shake off the affection, but they wish to shake it off as to have no desire to retain the money, or not; so that they desire only to wish for it or not according as God our Lord shall give them to wish, and according as it shall seem to them better for the service and praise of His Divine majesty; and meanwhile they wish to consider that they have in desire left all, striving to wish neither for this nor for any other thing, unless it be only the service of God our Lord that move them to this wish, so that the desire of being able the better to serve God our Lord is what moves them to take or leave the money."

In the example given by St. Ignatius, the men of this class aim at one objective: the service of God and their own salvation. Consequently, their affection toward money is already given up in their hearts. But how shall it be used? In whatever way that God wishes them to use it for His honor and glory.

In the beginning of this meditation I am bid, "to stand before God our Lord and all His saints, that I may desire and know that which is more pleasing to His Divine Goodness."

Granted that I have put myself in this position before God and all his saints, what is the effect on my soul? Any worldly considerations seem to vanish. God and His saints are interested in my welfare now, and I am bid to follow in their footsteps. I am begging to choose, "that which is most beneficial for the glory of His Divine Majesty and for the salvation of my own soul."

Here it should be noted that St. Ignatius is preparing an individual for the all important election of a state of life. However, if a person has already embraced the married or religious state of life, has this meditation any practical value? Yes, indeed. There may be some necessary adjustment in my life that requires a firm resolution to eliminate or to include some thing, and this could be a matter for election in a similar way to the actual choice of a state of life. Consequently, at the present time, our Divine Lord wants me to understand that no inordinate affection toward any creature whatsoever should stand between my complete conformity to His Holy Will. My reason has clearly shown to me the dangers implied in the first and second classes of men. Only as a member of the third class is it possible to love God as He wants to be loved. He may call me to make some sacrifice difficult for human nature, but He will help me to make it generously and with confidence. The example of the saints is my hope. "God loveth the cheerful giver" (2 Cor. 9, 7).

Now in conclusion I shall turn to the Blessed Mother asking her intercession for the grace I need. Then standing in spirit before our Blessed Lord, I shall offer my prayer in union with His own to God the Father: "Not my will but Thine be done."

The Election or Choice

As we saw previously in the Foundation, God is our final end, creatures are means to the end in so far as they are helpful. We likewise saw the necessity for indifference.

It frequently happens that we have to make a choice either regarding a very important matter as a state of life or other decisions which come up from time to time. Frequently it happens that decisions are made which are later regretted. It also happens that people become very confused over some matter and have serious difficulties in coming to any decision at all.

In order to help people make a permanent choice regarding their state in life or in making a satisfactory decision in some matter of lesser moment, St. Ignatius has formulated rules or suggestions which have been and will be very helpful. Consequently it will be profitable to read the exact text from the *Spiritual Exercises*.

If a person desires to make an Election regarding the choice of a state of life, it is advisable that this be done with the guidance of a spiritual director. The best time for choosing one's state of life is during a retreat.

PREPARATION FOR THE CHOICE

When a person is thinking about his or her choice of a state of life, what should be done? It is very essential to pray for light and guidance stressing a sincere desire of knowing God's Holy Will. "Dear Lord, what do You wish me to do?" Furthermore, one should be convinced that the choice is a strictly personal one. The advice of parents, relatives or teachers may be very helpful and encouraging, but in the final analysis their influence should not be decisive. Nor is self the only solution. How many have made the serious mistake of making a choice to please themselves. St. Ignatius warns against making this error. "As, for example, it happens that many choose first to marry, which is a means, and in the second place to serve God our Lord in the married state, which service of God is the end. So that these persons do not go straight to God...and consequently they make of an end a means, and of a means an end, so that what they ought to choose first, they choose last."

It is clear from this statement that a person about to choose a state of life should be free from inordinate af-fections, and moreover in a time of peace of soul, "in the time of calm when the soul is not agitated by diverse spirits, and uses its natural powers freely and calmly."

Let me consider a little child in the presence of a kind and loving father. If a child would be ready and willing to obey with confidence, shouldn't I be willing and ready to obey my heavenly Father with greater confidence?

The proper disposition of mind and humble child-like prayer are certainly the first steps toward making a choice of life...pleasing to God.

METHOD FOR MAKING THE CHOICE

In the meditation on the Kingdom of Christ, we saw the plan of the King. Remember? It is the plan for all who wish to follow Him as well as the motives for following Him, and the reward.

For a person who is about to make a final decision about a state in life, the question is resolved to this: I wish to follow my King in whichever state He calls me. I remain indifferent, that is, ready to follow His choice whether it be one state or another. This is my part, but I must remember a more important part; He is making a choice of me. "You have not chosen Me, but I have chosen you."

With this truth in mind, St. Ignatius calls for an intimate consultation between the servant and the King. I should, "beg of God our Lord that He may be pleased to move my will, and place in my soul that which I ought to do in regard to that which may be more to His praise and glory, considering the matter well and faithfully with my understanding, and choosing in conformity with His most holy will and good pleasure."

The very heart of the matter is the phrase, "that which

may be more to His praise and glory." After making the meditations on the Kingdom of Christ, the Two Standards, the Three Classes and the Three Degrees of Humility, we can have no doubt about making a choice that will be more to the praise and glory of God.

In conclusion, we come to four important rules of St. Ignatius that will help a person in choosing a state of life, or in making everyday decisions regarding family life, investments, various types of work, courses of study, help for the poor, aid for the missions etc.

"The first rule is that love, which urges and causes me to choose such or such a thing, descend from on high from the love of God; so that he who chooses, first feels in himself that the love which he has more or less for the thing he chooses, is solely for the sake of his Creator and Lord.

"The second rule is to place before my eyes a man whom I have never seen or known, and to consider what I, desiring all perfection for him, would tell him to do and choose for the greater glory of God our Lord, and the greater perfection of his soul; and acting so, to keep the rule which I lay down for another.

"The third rule is to consider, as if I were at the point of death, what would be the form and measure which I should then desire to have observed in the proceeding of the present election; and regulating my conduct according to this, I must make my decision in all things.

"The fourth rule is, viewing and considering what I shall then wish to have decided in regard to the present matter; and the rule which I should then wish to have observed, I will now observe, that I may then find myself full of joy and pleasure."

St. Ignatius then bids that the person who has made

the choice of life or decision "must with diligence betake himself to prayer, in the presence of God our Lord, and offer Him that election, that His Divine Majesty may be pleased to receive and confirm it, if it be to His greater service and praise."

Perhaps this little code may be used quickly in making some of the decisions of everyday life.

A .... Advice to another, follow yourself.
M .... My death. What would I do then?
D .... Day of judgment. Glad or sorry?
G .... Gratitude to God. He helped me.

The A M D G (*Ad majorem Dei gloriam*) means ... for God's greater glory! If my daily decisions are made with this motive in view, I will not be making mistakes, but real progress. There is so much sorrow and distress in the world because so many people have made the wrong selfish choice. Those who never regret the choice they have made are the real happy ones. They might have chosen differently but they chose something or someone with God in mind. For example: time for a retreat, a good confession, a Catholic school, a Catholic spouse, Sodality or Legion work, the right companions, good books, decent movies and parties. The real joy of it all is to feel that God Himself is pleased. Consequently upon a proper or improper choice will result whether I live with peace and joy in my heart or with sorrow and regret. Could anything be more safe-guarding and practical —than this little reflection? As a child to his Father, I will turn to Him and ask His guidance and strength not only to avoid temptation but to please Him, yes, even to the extent of seeking His greater honor and glory. Such is true unity—my soul with my Good Shepherd!

Reform of Life

In the words of St. Ignatius, all Spiritual Exercises are directed to the common goal, namely, "To conquer oneself and to regulate one's life, and to avoid coming to a determination through any inordinate affection." Once again we see that self conqest is a major objective. In the previous meditations this permanent objective has not lost its lustre. In fact it has become brighter through the basic and purifying meditations of the First Week, and the inspiring example of Christ during the Second Week.

What comes next? Before approaching the Third Week which is a period of strength and courage through meditations on the passion of Christ, St. Ignatius reverts to the main objective in part, "to regulate one's life" by proposing this important matter of Reform of Life and State.

When the state of one's life is determined, as in the religious, married or single state, it is surely God's will to amend and improve one's present life and state. He has called us to the highest perfection possible, "Be perfect as your heavenly Father is perfect." The saints have strived for perfection in every state of life. And we are called to do the same, in our respective state.

How shall I regulate my life? The first step is to look at it, and see if it isn't a bit out of focus. Perhaps we know from experience that no matter how expensive a camera may be, or how good the lens, or how beautiful the scene, if the camera is out of focus, the picture will be imperfect. By prayerful examination of conscience we are made aware of our many imperfections. With the help of God's grace we should try to correct our faults. It would be well to keep in mind this truth:

If you're not as near to God as you really should be, Remember ... *you* moved—Not He.

From the meditations on the End of Creatures and Personal sin I have certainly seen to what extent the picture of my life has been out of focus. God has been so good to me. As a result of those meditations or others, have I noted something in my life that should be eliminated? Maybe it is a bad habit regarding language, criticism of others, coming late for Mass. On the other hand, is there something positive that would make my life more pleasing to God, such as a little more considera- tion for others, more kindness, more generosity, more love, or whatever it may be.

Yes, whatever it may be, a sincere resolution will, if kept faithfully, make a decided change for the better. With this determination in mind, I will turn to our Blessed Lord asking His help and then apply to my resolution the four rules of St. Ignatius given at the end of the preceding consideration on the Election or Choice of life. The little code A. M. D. G. may act as a reminder of how I made my resolution and why I wish to keep it. Eternal salvation is my goal.

Now at this particular time, it is well to keep in mind the words of St. John Chrysostom:

"The more we lower ourselves
Through compassion,
The more closely do we come
To the things that are on high."

the
third
week

The Sorrowful Mysteries

The Last Supper

We have come to the Third Week of the *Spiritual Exercises*. Undoubtedly we have made a good resolution. Our Lord's passion and death will give us the grace to keep it. "Come to me, all you that labor and are heavily burdened and I will refresh you." How will He refresh us? By the sweet consolation of His passion for our sins. At this time we must bear in mind that Christ's sufferings are for us, for you and me personally.

The scene:

> Let us picture the apostles seated at the table with the Master. This is the great moment of His life by which His Divine Love is shared so intimately with our immortal souls. (Matt. 26, 17, 30).

The petition:

> Here I wish to ask for an even greater appreciation of the Holy Eucharist.

THE PREPARATION

"Where wilt Thou that we prepare for Thee to eat the Pasch?" The apostles are thoughtful of their Master. But our Lord, on His part was the one who was going to prepare something far greater than the Paschal feast. This was *His* hour, the time that He had looked forward to. He was to perform one more act in submission to the Old Law . . . to offer for the last time the Mosaic Sacrifice. The new sacrifice would be Himself.

There is a noticeable tension in the group as the usual ceremonies are gone through. What is in the mind of Judas? He cannot look at his Master, his head is downcast. He avoids every possible glance of the Master's eyes. He says nothing. The supper is ended.

"He riseth for supper and layeth aside His garments and having taken a towel, girded himself." What is He going to do? The apostles wonder, until they see their Master kneeling at their feet and washing them. And this is the Creator, God who has humbled Himself before His creatures, yes, even at the feet of Judas. What a lesson for me.

THE HOLY EUCHARIST

He instituted the Holy Eucharist as the greatest token of His love. The sole reason for His laying Himself upon the altar of sacrifice at the last Supper was His love. It was His way of remaining always with us, of being our Food and our Life.

"I will not leave you orphans." He knew how much we would need His strength and help. He saw that the Divine Food He would give us meant the Mass. He saw too that the Mass meant Calvary. He saw countless sacrilegious communions; He saw tabernacles being violated, the coldness of even priests and religious, and yet He went ahead with this sublime mystery.

Let us look devoutly at this scene for a moment. Christ is seated in the midst of the apostles. They watch Him intently as He takes the bread into His hands. They hear the words pronounced slowly and distinctly: "This is My Body." Where there had been a little piece of bread, there was now His Sacred Body, that on the morrow would be hanging on the cross. Then He took the chalice and in like manner blessed it and gave it to them after pronouncing the words: "This is My Blood of the New Testament." His precious Blood. One drop would have redeemed the world, but He desires to shed every drop for love of my soul.

But the marvel grows. Jesus added: "Do this for a commemoration of Me." A new ministry is confided to the apostles, a new priesthood is given. They are charged with the perpetuation of His miracle of love throughout all the ages and in all places of the world. "Oh, how great and honorable is the office given to priests, to consecrate with sacred words the Lord of majesty, to bless Him with their lips, to hold Him in their hands, to receive Him, and to give Him to others" (*Imitation,* Bk. 4, Ch. 11, 6).

I will pause for a moment, and place myself in the supper room and look into the face of Jesus. He has just performed the greatest of His miracles. Looking into those kindly eyes that seem to penetrate my soul, possessing as they do His kindness, forgiveness and love, I adore Him from the bottom of my heart: My Lord and my God.

HIS ETERNAL PROMISE

Speaking to the Jews our Lord had said: "He that eateth My Flesh and drinketh My Blood hath everlasting life and I will raise him up on the last day" (John, Ch. 6). He had changed water into wine at Cana. Now, at the last supper, He changes wine into His precious Blood, bread into His Adorable Body. At the very moment of this mystery of faith, He knew each one of us perfectly. I was just as present to His mind then as I am now. Yes, He knew each and every one of us individually. He knew the place and time of our First Holy Communion. He knew how many times we would receive Him during life. He saw our last communion on earth.

His words mean so much to the world today; they mean so much to me. "Come to Me all you that labor and are heavily burdened and I will refresh you...and you shall find rest for your souls." Here is the only answer for the upset world of today. But the world of our time will not listen, and so remains restless, self-seeking and discontented. Listen again to those words: "Come to Me... and you shall find rest for your souls." Perhaps or probably find rest? Our Lord said: "You will."

Holy Communion is the most beautiful union on earth. God and my soul. In taking ordinary food for the body, that food is assimilated and becomes a part of my body. But when I receive Holy Communion, this Food is infinitely stronger; it is Life Itself; it is the surest way to sanctity. Certainly then I must be careful in my preparation, and most grateful in my thanksgiving...for the greatest Gift upon earth, and the greatest pledge of life everlasting.

THE LIVING BREAD

These words of Jesus, "I am the Bread of Life"—are among the most revealing and consoling words He ever spoke. He is the *life* and *food* of our souls, the *bond* that unites us to Him, and the *pledge* of our eternal salvation. It is important to remember that our Holy Communions are not to be regulated by our feelings. Today we feel devout and pious and we approach the altar; another time we stay away from Communion because we are dry and distracted in prayer. This is a mistake. Our spiritual food must not be omitted because God has withheld His moments of consolation and fervor. He desires that Holy Communion be our frequent and even daily Bread. And with each Communion He brings to the individual soul exactly the grace that is needed. Above all others, the youth of today need His strength and friendship.

Although unable to comprehend this wonderful Mystery of God's love, we can thank Him for uniting our souls with Him now—as a pledge of eternal union in heaven.

Pour forth upon us, O Lord God, the spirit of Thy love, that by Thy mercy Thou mayest make those of one heart and mind whom Thou hast vouchsafed to feed with one heavenly Food. Through our Lord Jesus Christ, who liveth and reigneth with Thee in the unity of the same Holy Spirit, One God world without end. Amen.

The Agony in the Garden

First Sorrowful Mystery

The author of the Imitation says: "Many follow Jesus to the breaking of bread, but few to the drinking of the chalice of His passion." We have followed Him to the breaking of bread in our previous meditation, and now we are to follow Him in His passion, not merely as witnesses but in union with Christ suffering, with Christ heartbroken, to realize that what He suffers He suffers for me personally.

The scene:

Our Lord in the garden (Matt. 26, 30-46).

The petition:

To learn from Christ the meaning of suffering, and to ask for compassionate love.

ON THE WAY TO GETHSEMANE

He has offered Himself for sacrifice, and has given to His little flock His parting gift, "the greatest token of His love." He has told them of His love for them. Now let us follow our Lord as He leaves the cenacle and leads the way across the brook of Cedron into the garden of Gethsemane. He is strangely silent and sad. As they walk together in the moonlight, He tries to prepare them for what is coming, saying that they will be scandalized, shocked at the things that are going to happen that night, at the apparent failure of their King. He is likewise preparing me for the failures which are inevitably before me, because I have thrown in my lot with Him.

What were the thoughts of Christ as He walked along in the moonlight? Perhaps we can take the liberty to imagine at least one of them. As he glanced at the olive trees in the garden, did the thought of another tree in particular pass through His mind? Very likely. For somewhere in the vicinity of Jerusalem the tree had grown. Perhaps He had glanced at it frequently. And if so, He knew that the hour was approaching when He would stretch out His arms upon its branches, the tree of His cross. . . . In our lives it is only a little thing, and yet how significant, just a loving glance at our crucifix.

THE AGONY IN THE GARDEN

In the history of the world has there been any event to compare with our Lord's agony in the garden? He is outwardly calm, but inwardly . . . He tells them: "My soul is sorrowful unto death."

His hour had come. He took with Him His most intimate friends, Peter, James and John. Then He says to them: "stay you here and watch." He must leave even His three faithful apostles while He goes to pray to His Father. He went a little distance away and fell flat on the ground and prayed: "Father, all things are possible to Thee; remove this chalice from Me." From this prayer we can understand what the temptation was; not a temptation to sin, as it had been in the desert, but a temptation to go back upon the pledge He had made in the supper room, a temptation to take a lower standard, to save the world with less suffering. How vividly we are reminded of our meditation on the three classes of men and the third degree of humility. It is right here that my King fought the battle for me and gained the victory so that I might never take a low standard, or take back my former pledge of loyalty.

He was praying, we must remember, as a man, and as a man He went through the long and agonizing strife. Twice He went back to His three friends for sympathy, but each time they were asleep. They felt ashamed, but He excused them saying: "The spirit indeed is willing, but the flesh is weak."

And then comes the awful vision again, not one, but all the sins of the world. My sins and yours. He saw Himself covered with the sins of the world, and His body breaks out with a sweat of blood.

Perhaps what caused Jesus the most suffering in this terrible agony was the knowledge of the futility of it all for millions of souls. He saw those who would reject His Name, His religion, His apostles, and those who would abandon Him. We look and we listen to our Savior in His agony. What do we see? "His sweat became as drops of blood running down upon the ground" (Lk. 22, 44). And what do we hear from his sacred lips? "My Father, if this cup cannot pass away unless I drink it, thy will be done" (Matt. 26, 42). This act of obedience was made for each one of us. "For Jesus, in the days of his earthly life, with a loud cry and tears, offered up prayers and supplications to him who was able to save him from death, and was heard because of his reverent submission. And he, Son though he was, learned obedience from the things that he suffered; and when perfected, he became to all who obey him the cause of eternal salvation" (Heb. 5, 7-9).

And to think that we are individually in His mind

during all this suffering, even now while the blood is trickling down upon the ground. Surely if we could see Him now, we would cry out: "O, My God, it is enough, let Thy sufferings cease, it is not Your Sacred Blood but mine that should be shed for my sins."

And now we hear Him pray: "Father, if it be possible let this chalice pass from Me. However, not my will but Thine be done." The gospel says that He repeated the selfsame prayer. Was it necessary for Him to do so. No. He is teaching me the lesson of perseverance. When prayer was an agony to St. Isaac Jogues he cut a cross upon a tree and gazed at it. What does the crucifix mean to me? No one is ever holy without suffering in union with Christ.

THE BETRAYAL BY JUDAS

While Christ was sweating blood in agony and the apostles were asleep, the enemies of Christ were very busy. Our Lord returns to His apostles. "Rise up, let us go. Behold, he that will betray Me is at hand." As they rose up to go with Him, they could see the lanterns and torches and the glittering weapons among the trees. Our Lord walked straight toward His enemies, the servants of the Hight Priest, the officers appointed by the Sanhedrin, and the Roman soldiers who were there in case of a riot. With the servants and officers Judas came forward to meet Him. "And Jesus said: 'Friend whereto art thou come?' He answered, 'Hail, Master,' and He kissed Him," thus giving the prearranged sign for which he received the thirty pieces of silver and bartered his soul.

But Christ did not shrink from the embrace of Judas.

He called him "Friend." There was no response to this final plea of friendship, no humility, no repentance. The crime is consummated. One sin more, an act of despair, and Judas will plunge into the eternal darkness of hell. This was one of God's chosen few, one of the twelve, who, had he corresponded with grace, would have become St. Judas.

"Then his disciples leaving Him all fled away." They had seen His divinity. They had received His sacred body and blood, and yet, what cowards. They had promised, and even repeatedly sworn to be faithful to Him even unto death. They heard His voice commanding His enemies not to touch any of them. But in spite of this, fear overcame them, self must be saved. How many times have we done this same thing. We have made a resolution and we desire to keep it, but after a time, self-love begins to feel the hurt, and the fidelity which we promised to Christ is put aside for some gratification of self.

Finally, we see our Lord bound and led away through the darkness, to bear His suffering alone.

O my suffering Savior, it was for me that You went through Your agony in the garden. All my sins were present before You. But now I sincerely repent for all my sins. Even as You walked alone abandoned by your apostles in Gethsemane, You witnessed me also at this hour making a meditation on Your agony. Let me now be faithful in following Your footsteps although I know it will mean sharing in Your cross. My prayer is now the "Anima Christi":

> Soul of Christ, sanctify me.
> Body of Christ, save me.

Blood of Christ, inebriate me.
Water from the side of Christ, wash me.
Passion of Christ, strengthen me.
O good Jesus, hear me.
Within Thy wounds, hide me.
Permit me not to be separated from Thee.
From the malignant enemy defend me.
In the hour of my death call me,
And bid me come to thee,
That, with thy saints, I may praise Thee
Forever and ever, Amen.

Christ is Taken to the High Priest

It must have been midnight, or even after, when the tribune with his band of soldiers and the servants of the Jews led their Captive in chains from the garden to the high priest Annas. A meditation is something very personal and just as we tried to realize that He became incarnate for us, now we must try to realize that He is suffering for us. Consequently we say to ourselves: "The least that I can do is to stand by my King."

The scene:

Try to picture the innocent Jesus before Annas, Caiphas and the Sanhedrin (John 18, 13-40).

The petition:

Here I will beg the grace to stand by my King although tempted constantly by the world, the flesh and the devil.

BEFORE ANNAS, THE HIGH PRIEST

Their captive gave them no trouble. Here we keep before our eyes the meek and humble Jesus. He is being led as a convict, but we are the ones who are really guilty. Each step that He takes is one of love for us. How our Lord is teaching us to be patient under the trials of life.

Today there are many missionaries suffering from severe persecution. Be it mental, physical or spiritual, let us remember to pray for them.

His captors are triumphant and want to show their Prisoner to Annas, who knows of course that the Sanhedrin has sent them to capture Jesus and has been awaiting their arrival with some curiosity. Annas proceeds to question our Lord about His teaching and His followers, for he intends his verdict to be against Christ and he hopes to find some excuse for it.

Jesus answered him: "I have spoken openly to the world; I have always taught in the synagogue, and in the temple whither the Jews resort; and in secret I have spoken nothing. Why askest thou Me? Ask them who have heard what I have spoken unto them; behold they know what things I have said."

And when He had said these things, one of the servants standing by gave Jesus a blow saying: "Answerest thou the high priest so?"

Jesus answered him: "If I have spoken evil, give testimony of the evil; but if well, why strikest thou Me?" And today He could add: "Why strikest thou My Church?"

If we should ever be insulted, here is the fact to

remember—our Lord was struck in the face. He remains calm; there is nothing more to say against Him. Annas has failed in his purpose. There is only one thing to do, hand Jesus over to the guards while waiting for the gathering of the Sanhedrin.

What, we may ask, was Peter doing at this time? Where was he while Christ was being struck in the face? Peter was in some other part of the courtyard "warming himself." Once again, it is the question of seeking self instead of Christ.

CHRIST BEFORE CAIPHAS

"Annas then sent Him bound to Caiphas the high priest." First, let us enter the palace of Caiphas, the hall where the Sanhedrin is gathered on that early morning of the first Good Friday. Caiphas, the worldly priest, who has subordinated the eternal to the temporal, the spiritual to the material, and who does not live for the faith but makes a livelihood out of it, and who tries to do the impossible, to serve God and the world. Caiphas is surrounded by men of this type.

And there in the midst of them stands Christ. He has taught that the supreme task of religion is to love everybody, even one's enemies, and that the sacrifice most pleasing to God is the sacrifice of a pure heart. He has preferred little children and poor fishermen to the proud doctors of the law, and instead of the temporal and powerful Messiah they expect, He has come to us poor, humble and despised. So He stands now before those who have plotted against His life by the use of false witnesses. At last Caiphas puts the tremendous question to Him:

"I adjure Thee by the living God that Thou tell us if Thou be the Christ, the Son of God."

Christ declares that He is the Son of God. The entire life of Christ was directed toward this great revelation.

"Thou hast said it," He replied. "Nevertheless, I say to you, hereafter you shall see the Son of Man sitting on the right hand of the power of God, and coming in the clouds of heaven."

Then the high priest rent his garments saying: "He hath blasphemed. What further need have we of any witnesses? Behold now you yourselves have heard the blasphemy; what think you?" They had indeed heard the truth and there were those among them who on the very next afternoon would come down from the hill of Calvary, fearfully crying: "Indeed this was the Son of God."

But now is their hour of decision. "What think you?" said Caiphas, and they answered: "He is guilty of death." Christ is condemned to death for telling the truth. Does my conscience reproach me for untruthfulness?

CHRIST BEFORE PILATE AND HEROD

Caiphas sends our Lord to the governor in order to have the sentence of death approved.

Christ comes before Pilate. What was it that Pilate heard the mob saying when asked about Christ? "We have found this Man perverting our nation and forbidding to give tribute to Caesar and saying that He is Christ the King." The last charge was one of treason and Pilate could not dare to let it pass by. Pilate said to Him: "Art thou the king of the Jews?" And Christ answered: "My kingdom is not of this world."

Listen to these words of Christ: "Everyone that is of the truth heareth my voice."

Pilate asked the question: "What is truth?" Pilate asks the right question for the wrong reasons. The answer stood before him.

That is the question that men have been asking ever since the time of Pilate. Some have found the answer, and fortunately so for themselves and others. What is our Catholic heritage except the truth. And the Truth is Christ Himself. "I am the way, the truth, and the life." But Pilate paid no attention to what Christ might reply to his question. He leaves the pretorium hurriedly, faces the people and says: "I find no cause in Him." Pilate would not condemn Him, but his desire for popularity prevented him from setting the prisoner free.

Then they were more earnest saying: "He stirreth up the people, teaching thoughout all Judea, beginning from Galilee even to this place." Even the good that Christ did is now turned against Him. His miracles, His kindness, His compassion.

And so Pilate brings Jesus before the people. "Behold the man." Crowned with thorns, His face covered with spittle, a dirty purple cloak about His torn shoulders. His body one great throbbing pain. "Behold the man."

No, He is more than man. He is my King and my Leader. Oh, Jesus I adore You. I accept You. I will hate what the world loves and embraces, and seek what You love and embrace. Let worldly men seek honors, pleasures, and the credit of a great name. I will delight in being like You, my King. I will follow You just as You are. I love You just as You are, my King!

Pilate rejoiced when he heard the name of Galilee. He would be under Herod's jurisdiction, so Christ is next taken to the court of the vain sensual Herod, the murderer of John the Baptist. Herod asks a few questions, but our Lord makes no reply. What kind of treatment does my King receive? "Herod with his army set Him at nought and mocked Him and put on Him a white garment of fools. What a humiliation. But our Lord could say: "Learn of Me because I am meek and humble of heart."

Our blessed Lord is brought back to Pilate. It is the custom of the feast to release a prisoner and Pilate asks the people whether to release Barabbas or Jesus. Again the King is to suffer this humiliation of having a criminal preferred before Him.

And now the final outrage takes place. Christ is taken out to be scourged. His flesh gradually becomes livid beneath the blows of the lash; gaping wounds appear and blood streams forth from His sacred body. The silent patience and meekness of the divine Victim only increases their savage cruelty.

I must always keep in mind that Christ suffered His passion because He loved me personally. At least, do I begin to understand something of His tremendous love for my soul? What is my response? At times even a harsh word arouses my anger, and if I sense that some injustice has been done to me, how different is my reaction to that of the patient Jesus. Compassionate Savior, teach me daily to offer my little sufferings in union with your passion and death.

Conclude with the "Anima Christi."

The Scourging at the Pillar

Second Sorrowful Mystery

In meditating on the passion of our Lord, I should always keep in mind that whatever Jesus suffers He does so for me personally. The scourging of Christ was one of the most cruel deeds His enemies could inflict. It had been foretold centuries previously that our Lord would be so wounded for our sins that we would have thought Him "as it were a leper and as one struck by God and afflicted" (Isaiah 53, 4). This prophecy was now fulfilled at the word of Pilate.

The scene:

Witness our blessed Lord at the pillar, stripped and beaten so cruelly that His sacred body was covered with His precious blood (John 19, 1).

The petition:

To ask for the grace never to offend Christ by sins of the flesh, in thought, word or deed.

CHRIST CONDEMNED

Among the Jews, scourging usually preceded crucifixion. But Pilate hoped that in the case of Christ the scourging alone would be sufficient to appease the people. Listen to his words: "I, having examined Him before you, find no cause in this man in those things wherein you accuse Him. I will chastise Him therefore and release Him" (Luke 18, 14-16).

Here was the most illogical and unjust sentence a man could pronounce, summarized in the single word "therefore." Pilate proclaimed Christ to be innocent, *therefore* He should be free if logic means anything. But Pilate wasn't thinking about logic, he was thinking about himself. He was smart enough to know that had he stood by Christ firmly he would have lost his popularity with the Jews, his reputation, his job. No, Pilate could not let anything interfere with himself.

Looking back, we condemn such weaklings as Pilate, the politician, and Herod the tyrant, both proclaiming Christ innocent and yet acting otherwise. And what of the world today? In great part, the world claims to be Christian and yet continues like Pilate to scourge and like Herod to dishonor Christ by sin.

Now I shall look closely at my Savior and note how He accepts this unjust condemnation. He was accepting more than an unjust sentence, He was accepting the "chalice" from His Father for the salvation of the very people who were conspiring against Him. Even now, His heart was saying: "Father, forgive them."

Like her founder, Christ, the Church has always been condemned. Today the persecution surpasses that of any former period of history. It is not merely human hatred against Christ and His Church but diabolical hatred. Satan cannot strike against God, so he concentrates his forces against the image of God in the person of cardinals, archbishops, bishops, priests, brothers, nuns, and countless members of the laity. How are they accepting the "chalice"? Thank God, in imitation of Christ they are offering their sufferings for the conversion of their Communistic persecutors. Their hearts are also repeating a prayer: "Father forgive them."

As a Catholic, I must expect to be condemned from time to time, that is, if I am trying to live my faith. From whatever source the persecution may come, I too must be mindful of the words of our Lord Himself: "Blessed shall you be when men shall hate you, and when they shall separate you and shall reproach you and cast out your name as evil for the Son of Man's sake. Be glad and rejoice in that day, for behold your reward is great in heaven" (Luke 6, 22-23).

THE SCOURGING

I shall try to witness the scene as it actually took place. Amid infamous blasphemies, our Lord is stripped of the seamless tunic which He wears. It had been made for Him by the gentle hands of His mother. Now it is roughly torn from Him by the brutal hands of His tormentors and our Lord stands uncovered while He is bound to a pillar. Then, in rapid succession, the cruel blows fall upon His virginal body. His flesh is torn until the bones are exposed. The scourging in the face and across His shoulders and back is extremely painful because these parts are so full of sensitive and delicate nerves. Meanwhile a pool of blood is gathering on the floor, His precious Blood, of which one little drop would have redeemed the world.

In my meditation I must not shrink from this scene but rather come closer, realizing to the full Who the victim is that is being so barbarously and ignominiously treated. It is the Lord, the Creator of heaven and earth, the omnipotent God. And why is He suffering this terrible scourging? Because He wishes to save me from the grievous and eternal torments that my sins have deserved. O infinite love of God!

Why, I may ask, does He suffer so intensely throughout all the members of His body? Christ is suffering for the countless sins of the flesh. The same warning could be given today as at Fatima: "The sins that lead most men to hell are the sins of the flesh."

Now again, witnessing our Lord so cruelly scourged at the pillar, what are my feelings except heartfelt gratitude joined with sincere contrition for my sins? I should also turn to His mother, for I have caused her sorrow too. She understood more intimately than anyone else, how deep were the mental and physical sufferings of her divine Son. When appearing at Fatima, our Lady of the Rosary uttered this solemn warning to all: "I have come to warn the faithful to amend their lives and ask pardon for their sins. They must not continue to offend our Lord, who is already so deeply offended."

SINCERE AMENDMENT

By the mercy of God we are given the opportunity to amend our lives, and nothing could be more important in His sight. Christ is our Redeemer, our hope. Good Friday is the prelude to Easter; amendment is the prelude to forgiveness.

We are definitely associated with our Lord in the suffering prior to His death. He came into the world, took flesh, became one of us, in order to bear the burden of human sin. In His hours of suffering we were there. We took part in that cruel scourging at the pillar. But

O, how sorry I am for my sins. Life has come to my soul through His Precious Blood.

In my prayer now, I will take my place near our Lord suffering at the pillar. My God, I believe, I adore, I hope in, I love you. I ask pardon for all those who do not believe, or adore, or hope in, or love You. I am heartily sorry for all my sins and wish to make amendment to Your Sacred Heart.

The Crowning with Thorns

Third Sorrowful Mystery

As the scourging at the pillar was in reparation for the sins of the flesh, so the crowning of thorns was in atonement for the sins of the mind. God's wonderful gifts to man, the faculties of his soul, intellect, understanding, memory, and will, have been constantly abused. There are those who openly disclaim God, deny His very existence, others who deny the doctrine and the divinity of Christ, and still others who have tried and are still trying to crush the idea of God through an attempt to substitute the false gods of materialism, egotism and worldly power. Christ suffered for all the sins of the mind, by having His head pierced cruelly with thorns.

The scene:

See our Blessed Lord crowned with thorns, ridiculed and mocked as a false king (John 19, 2-5).

The petition:

Ask for the grace not to offend God by consenting to sinful thoughts.

THE MOCK KING

The barbarous gang of torturers, being tired at last with scourging our Lord, untie Him from the pillar. What do I see? Can I recognize Jesus so covered with gaping wounds? He is completely exhausted by the loss of so much blood and is left completely alone to seek out and pick up His clothes. So, mangled by their barbarity, hardly able to help Himself, He clothes His body as well as possible. But the pain is only increased. The coarse woolen garments rub against those fresh wounds at every step and motion. And this is God suffering at the hand of His own creatures. What cruel abuse of human hands, and yet men and women continue to commit sins today by hands that were made to do good.

What greater torment could these barbarians possibly think of? Satan is the master of cruelty, and he is never finished. What thoughts of evil could he suggest now? Make of Christ a mock-king. Yes, put a crown of thorns upon His head. Press it down so that the sharp points would penetrate His skull. Put in His hands a reed for scepter, and then go to the very extreme: Kneel before Him in humiliating mockery; pay Him homage; salute Him with the words: "Hail, king of the Jews." And then, by turns, these men buffet Him, and spit in His face, and strike Him over the head, causing the thorns to penetrate deeper until the blood trickles down His face. And this is my Savior, Jesus, bearing all of this in patience and silence for the love of my soul. In this hour of agony, I adore Him, my true King.

"In Christ's suffering," Pope Paul has said, sorrow becomes sacred." We listen to the Holy Father's words,

"It is the patient Christ, the great brother of everyone who is poor and who suffers, Who gave human sorrow its super human character. The object of respect, care and veneration, Christ does not only show the dignity of sorrow. Christ calls for a vocation of sorrow." Christ alone teaches me the meaning of suffering.

THE TRUE KING

This awful scene of derision had been foreseen and foretold by our Lord when He said to the apostles: "Behold we go up to Jerusalem, and the Son of man shall be betrayed to the chief priests, and to the scribes and ancients, and they shall condemn Him to death. And they shall mock Him and spit on Him, and scourge Him and kill Him" (Mark 10, 33-34).

Such infamous treatment of our Divine Lord has won for many in our own day the grace to remain faithful even unto death. Christ chose to be without defence. He deliberately chose humiliation and suffering. What do I choose? If I am too weak to choose humiliation, do I at least accept it when it comes? To be Christlike, self must suffer.

Looking again at Christ, battered and bruised, I recognize my true king for what He is, the Savior of those who have fallen to the depths of inhumanity in thought and word and deed. Would our Lord have forgiven their devilish thoughts? Yes. Would He have forgiven their words of blasphemy and mockery? Certainly. Would He have forgiven everything, including the cruel crown of thorns? Yes, everything. But nobody asked to be forgiven. Three sincere words from the lips of the lowest would have saved these sinful creatures from the just punishment they deserved: "Lord, forgive me."

Our true king tells all alike: "I have overcome the world." Yes, He has overcome the malice, the wickedness, the sins of mankind. His passion and death have conquered pride and the other capital sins. No man need ever feel that he has fallen too low or that he has been away from his religious duties too long to be forgiven by Christ. It is never too late to ask for forgiveness.

Now, in my prayer, realizing more fully how much our Lord suffered for my sins, I will again ask His pardon from the motive of love, and beg pardon, too, for those who have not asked to be forgiven. I shall conclude with the "Anima Christi."

The Way of the Cross

Fourth Sorrowful Mystery

"And bearing His own cross, Jesus went forth to that place which is called Calvary." Here I shall witness the tremendous love of Christ for souls.

The scene:

I shall follow my King along the sorrowful road to Calvary and try to realize that every step was taken for the love of my immortal soul.

The petition:

I shall ask for the grace to carry my own cross in union with my Savior.

THE VIA DOLOROSA

Jesus, crushed and battered as He was from the scourging and the terrible treatment at the hands of the soldiers, had the courage to welcome the cross with open arms and heart. The tree that He had probably looked upon many a time in the garden was now in His arms. He had already done far more than enough to redeem mankind, but He desired to be obedient unto death, even to the death of the cross. At this time He visioned all those who would reject the cross during the centuries to come, and those who would carry it faithfully, even lovingly.

A man's greatness is often measured by his response to failure. The cross of Christ was considered as a sign of failure by many of His own time—and many today. Looked upon as the means of our eternal salvation, the cross of Christ means true and lasting victory. Blessed be the cross of Christ as I now visualize His passion in my meditation.

Here I shall picture the familiar scenes as though actually present. As I look, therefore, upon the disfigured face of Jesus, I shall see the penetrating eyes of my Savior searching the depths of my soul; only two words cross His lips: "For you." Yes, He is doing this for me personally. He is the innocent one; I am the guilty sinner. And yet, by this very cross He is making me innocent; He is taking away my sins. But at what a price. After a few faltering steps, our Lord is crushed to the ground beneath the heavy burden.

JESUS MEETS HIS MOTHER

This was one of the saddest meetings that ever took place. He has been pulled up on His feet again and has now reached the spot where His mother is standing. They do not say anything but they understand without words. The soldiers do not let Him remain, but push Him forward. All this He suffers patiently, not for Himself but for me. And the best I can do is to follow along, thankful for the honor of walking beside the mother of my Redeemer. Her eyes are cast downwards, watching the road lest she step on the drops of His Precious Blood.

There are many others who follow Jesus. It is His desire to save them all, and yet there are those present whose sole aim is to put Him to death. And to make certain that He will die upon the cross and not before, Simon of Cyrene is called upon to help Jesus carry the cross.

Strange that one of the apostles didn't offer to do that. Once so brave, now so timid. But let me rather look to myself than blame the apostles. How many times have I refused to carry the cross, even some little mortification, some slight humiliation?

If anyone sincerely feels that he would have liked to assist our Lord in some way during that first way of the cross, then he should listen to these words: "If any man will come after Me, let him deny himself and take up his cross daily and follow Me." We are all given the chance to carry the cross, but we will never have the courage or strength to carry it alone. We must carry our cross in union with Christ.

Again I must follow Jesus in this sorrowful journey. There is one friend in the crowd who pushes her way closer to Him. It is Veronica, the holy woman who wipes the face of Jesus. What a kind thought on her part. And what a kind deed. Through the kindness of Veronica, the image of this sacred Face is preserved even to the present day.

There is no record that our Lord spoke to His mother, to Simon or to Veronica during this tiresome journey, But He is touched by the sympathy of the women of Jerusalem. They were weeping for Him and I can hear the words He addresses to them: "Daughters of Jerusalem, weep not for Me but for yourselves and for your children." Even in this extreme moment of suffering, Jesus is not thinking of Himself but of others.

And finally, after this sorrowful climb to Calvary, we reach the place of execution. He has completed His Way of the Cross to the summit of Calvary. In our day and for us it is the Royal Road of the Cross, for it is the way that our King has deliberately chosen for Himself. And what does this choice of His mean to us? St. Peter gives us the answer: "Unto this, indeed, you have been called, because Christ also has suffered for you, leaving you an example that you may follow in his steps (1 Pet. 2. 21). I look again at the cross in the arms of Christ and I offer to Him my prayer of sincere thanksgiving for His loving journey of redemption. In union with Jesus I will follow the Way of the Cross with greater devotion, and conclude my meditation now with the "Anima Christi."

The Crucifixion

Fifth Sorrowful Mystery

In this meditation I shall spend the time on the Mount of Calvary witnessing the Divine Victim offering His life for the salvation of the world. But to grasp the full meaning of His personal love, I must realize that His sufferings and death on the cross were offered willingly for my soul. "I lay down my life.... No man taketh it away from me ... but I lay it down of myself" (John 10, 17-18).

The scene:

> To witness the scene of Calvary with attention to every detail in a spirit of faith and compassion (Luke 23, 32-33).

The petition:

> To ask the grace of a greater love of Christ's passion and death.

CHRIST IS NAILED TO THE CROSS

O, so difficult a climb for Jesus to the mountain top. Finally the condemned men and their executioners arrive at the place called Calvary. Did the Cyrenian help our Lord to the very end? Let us hope he did.

The executioners pull the ragged garments from His wounds and the mob sees for the first time the terrible wounds as a result of the scourging. His Precious Blood is flowing from many places.

Now He is pushed downward upon the cross. A few rough men have already grabbed His garments. In this pitiable and helpless condition our Lord has strength enough to stretch forth His hands on the cross. His hand is pulled open and a rough nail is held in place. Then as I wait near His mother, I too hear the awful sound of the hammer striking the nail. Jesus is offering this terrible suffering to His Father and I know that Mary is doing the same. Again, the cruel sound of the hammer and the other hand is nailed...for my sins.

Jesus, willing to let His humanity suffer, seems able to do nothing. He is helpless in body, but O! how active in soul. Every moment of suffering is another moment of love. Here in my meditation I will pause to realize how much our Lord, nailed to the cross, helpless and suffering, has meant to thousands of souls. The martyrs of the past have received their courage and strength from Him as do the martyrs of today.

We hear of many who are helpless in Red prisons; others are helpless in hospitals, some are confined in ironlungs, many are paralyzed. What a little glance at the crucifix means to these souls! They alone know how much it does mean. They see Jesus nailed hand and foot. Each one may say in their hearts: this He did for me, and now I am returning love for love. Souls are saved in union with Christ suffering.

CHRIST UPON THE CROSS

Now the cross is raised up momentarily and then jolted down into the earth. I raise my eyes. There is Christ my beloved Savior suspended between heaven and earth. Hanging by nails pierced through His flesh! His mother takes her place now at the foot of the cross; though so unworthy, I will do the same. My Jesus mercy.

Without being fully aware of it, the mob stands and watches the greatest conflict the world has ever known. The battle for heaven and against hell is intensified. The first man, Adam, by disobedience to the command of God, shut the gates of heaven to Himself and His children and threw open the gates of hell. But the heavenly Father in His Divine Mercy promised a champion, a redeemer, who would forever open the gates of heaven, and who would also crush forever the power of hell. That hour, that long awaited hour had come. It came now.

The first woman in her pride had sought to rob God, but now the new Eve stands humbly beneath the cross. Her tender love for souls is shown here on Calvary every second. She is offering to God the Father, the life of His only Son and her own. And the people stand watching.

How easily this mob is led! And the pity is that millions are being led today by the few who would crucify Christ again if they could. Here on Calvary, what do the few incite the mob to shout? "If thou be the Son of God, come down from the cross!" He is offering them salvation and they shout, "come down!"

But Jesus remained on the cross. Never would He compromise with the world to come down and make a false peace. The world at large has not learned the lesson of the cross, and consequently the Catholic Chuch as a whole and individual members in particular, are often criticized because of their high standards of Christian life. Satan is always active with his suggestions to come down to a lower standard of ease and pleasure and to disregard self denial. And at what a cost? Only a false peace of conscience is the result, which, in reality, means no peace at all.

My attention is upon Christ crucified. O, how significant are the outstretched arms of Jesus. Even as a babe, His tiny arms were outstretched to Mary and Joseph. Later in life, He welcomed the little ones with outstreched arms. And with this same kindly gesture, He fed the multitudes, lifted the lame, restored the sick to health and the dead to life. Finally with outstretched arms He embraced the cross and now they are outstretched to the limit and bleeding. As He lived, so He dies with His loving arms extended to the souls He came to save.

Today the priest at the altar renews the sacrifice of Christ on Calvary. How privileged I am to offer Mass in union with all the faithful who are present. Please grant to me, my Savior an ever increasing love of Your sacrifice, the Holy Sacrifice of the Mass.

Now in spirit at the foot of the cross I will recite, "The Prayer to Jesus Crucified," and with this prayer offer my own little cross in union with that of my Savior.

Look down upon me, good and gentle Jesus, while before Thy Face I humbly kneel, and with burning soul pray and beseech Thee to fix deep in my heart lively sentiments of Faith, Hope, and Charity, true contrition for my sins, and a firm purpose of amendment; while I contemplate with great love and tender pity Thy five wounds, pondering over them within me, and calling to mind what the prophet David put in Thy mouth concerning Thee, O Good Jesus: "They have pierced my hands and feet; they have numbered all my bones." Amen. (Ps. 21, 17-18)

The First Word

"Father, forgive them, for they know not what they do."

The eyes of the entire mob were focused upon Christ. The cursing and blasphemy stopped. The crucified King was opening His lips. Would that silent tongue now cry out in pain? They had heard the cries of the crucified before. Yes, they expected a cry of agony and despair such as they had often heard before from the victims of torture. But this was not the kind of cry that they heard. From the depth of His loving heart came less a cry than a prayer, a soft, gentle prayer of pardon and forgiveness. "Father, forgive them for they know not what they do."

Forgive whom? Forgive enemies? Yes, all of them. The soldier in the court room who had struck Him with a clenched fist; Pilate the politician who had condemned Him in order to retain the friendship of Caesar...and all the other Pilates of the world.

Forgive whom? Forgive Caiphas who refused to believe in the Son of God...and forgive, Father, all the other atheists the world over "for they know not what they do."

Forgive whom? Forgive Peter, and with him all the others who have denied Me. Peter had said, "I know not the man." Forgive them all, Father, who have falsely denied My Divinity...." For they know not what they do."

Forgive whom? All of my executioners. Those who have pierced my hands and feet; they have numbered my Body, and all those in the future who will desecrate the Sacrament of my Love. Those who will destroy my churches, break open my tabernacles, and stamp upon my sacred Body. "Forgive them, Father, for they know not what they do."

Forgive those also who have caused Me pain. Those who have beaten Me with their whips and those who caused the beating by their sins of sensuality and impurity. Turning to their bodies in sinful pleasure, they have made my Body a mass of wounded flesh. Forgive those who have crowned My head with thorns with their evil thoughts and desires and who have caused My eyes to smart and sting by looking at sinful objects.

Forgive those, too, who have cracked and puffed my lips by their words of blasphemy, their sinful use of My Holy Name, their words of anger, cursing, and swearing. ..."For they know not what they do."

Forgive those who have stripped Me of My garments by their immodesty, their immoral dress and behavior. Those who have pierced My hands by their sins of impure touch. Those who have pierced my feet by walking into places of sin.

We learn from this first word of Christ upon the cross that there is no limit to pardon. Here we see the Son of God, beloved of the Father, holding back by His outstretched arms the just wrath of His Father.

We learn from this first word of Christ upon the cross that there is no limit to pardon. Here we see the Son of God, beloved of the Father, holding back by His outstretched arms the just wrath of His Father.

How can I, a sinner, ever hold back forgiveness? Christ held back nothing, not even a single drop of His Precious Blood.

Teach me, O my Jesus crucified to forgive. Teach me to forgive today even the smallest injury, because they are all so small in comparison with Yours. Above all, dear Jesus, let me never forget my sins and what suffering they caused you there upon the cross. In your first word is salvation, the beautiful word that only you could have spoken: "Father, forgive them, for they know not what they do."

The Second Word

"Amen I say to you, this day thou shalt be with me in paradise."

On the hill of Calvary stood not one cross, but three. With Christ our Lord were crucified two sinners one on the left and one on the right. And though they would have fled this dreaded moment, even as we might flee our own cross, each man hung upon his cross in pain and misery.

They both heard what the mob shouted to the Innocent One between them. "If thou be the Son of God, come down from the cross." While the shouting and blasphemy continued, the criminal on the left joined his angry voice with the rabble.

He envied the power which our Blessed Lord had claimed. As the chief priests, scribes, and pharisees shouted beneath the cross, "He saved others, himself He cannot save," the thief on the left added to their revilings, "If thou be the Christ, save thyself and us," In other words he was saying: "If I had that power that you claim as the Messiah, I would use it differently than to hang there helpless. I would step down from the cross, smite my enemies and prove what power really is." Looking only to self he failed.

The criminal on the right, however, was moved at seeing Jesus suffering without complaint and even praying for the forgiveness of His executioners. Then the good thief turning to the other thief said, "Neither dost thou fear God seeing thou art under the same condemnation? And we indeed justly, for we receive the due reward of our deeds; but this man hath done no evil."

Then turning to Christ, he made one of the most sublime acts of faith ever recorded. Addressing Christ nailed to the cross, abandoned by His followers, reviled by His own people and realizing that the mob below would only jeer and ridicule his words, he lifted his eyes and said to Jesus, "Lord, remember me when thou shalt come into thy kingdom."

Amid all the confusion and shouting, that one act of faith penetrated the heart of Christ. Here was the first fruit of His redeeming sacrifice. Then He spoke those words of complete pardon which transformed a hardened criminal into a repentant saint. And Jesus said to him, "Amen, I say to thee, this day thou shalt be with me in paradise." With these words our Lord canonized the first saint. The good thief proclaimed Christ to be a King. Although, our Lord was most pleased with the faith of the good thief, He did not remove him from the cross as He could have done. Nor at this moment would the penitent sinner have wished it otherwise. His cross was the key to heaven.

And the people stood watching these three. The dying Savior of mankind hung watching also. In vision He saw all those who would accept the cross and those who would not. He saw your soul and mine.

Because He knew the future perfectly as God, He was watching us as we go through life carrying our cross. Whether in sickness or poverty, the pain of unfaithfulness, or unkindness, or the sorrow caused by the loss of a dear one. Jesus saw everything. He sees us stumble and fall in our struggle against the world, the flesh and the devil. He sees us rise with His help. He sees the effect of His cross and our own upon the future. Yes, through His saving cross, and the fidelity in accepting our own in union with His, victory will come!

The sufferings to which an angry God once condemned rebellious man, are now the precious treasures whereby man may attain his salvation. The cross we carry is a reminder of the cross of Christ. "Thy sorrow shall be turned into joy." We cannot escape suffering, but we can make it our most powerful prayer. God will accept our share in His cross. May I ever unite my will to His...whose Will is always one of love.

> I know not by
> what method rare,
> But this I know,
> God answers prayer.
> I know not when He sends the word
> That tells me fervent prayer is heard;
> I know it cometh soon or late,
> My part is but to pray and wait.
> I know not if the blessing sought
> Will come in just the guise I thought.
> I leave all care with Him above,
> Whose Will is always one of love.

The Third Word

"Woman, behold thy son....Behold thy mother."

As the strange shadows of gloom hung low over the cross, the crowds began to thin out, terrified at the unwonted happening. The faithful were grouped near the cross, His Mother, Magdalen, and John. "When Jesus therefore had seen His mother and the disciple standing whom He loved, He said to His mother: "Woman, behold thy son." After that He saith to His disciple: "Behold thy mother."

Has generosity such as this ever been met with elsewhere? Here I will make the effort to comprehend to some degree what Christ actually did when speaking to His mother and John. Besides His few garments, Christ had nothing of material value during His lifetime. He wrote nothing, He shared the work of preaching with His apostles and eventually left the whole of that ministry with them. The one thing which He determined to reserve for Himself was suffering. His work seemed a failure; many of His friends disappeared, but He still had His mother. Now, out of love for mankind, He gives up His mother, or rather shares her with us as if to say to Mary: "Help Me in My work; take the souls of mankind for your children; be a mother to all. Woman, behold they son, thy children, all the children of Eve."

Then to John and to us He says: "Behold thy mother," as if to say: "Accept my mother to care for you. The purest creature ever made I chose for my mother and now I give her to you. Go to her for all you wish. I cannot refuse her intercession. She is my mother. Learn from her the way to heaven. Behold my mother . . . she is also yours."

Christ chose to suffer this final pain of separation from His mother that He might atone for the sins committed against the holiness of the family and the little ones. He bears this pain in order that the little ones who are deprived of their parents and neglected may bear their sorrow.

Behold thy mother. Mary, the Refuge of Sinners, had long known what would be the end for her divine Son; she had no delusions like the apostles concerning the "kingdom." The grace that filled her soul gave her a capacity for suffering that we cannot comprehend. Only a mother can know the sufferings of a mother. Only the mother of God can know much of the sufferings that racked the heart of Christ.

Mary knew the horror of sin; she knew what agony men were causing her Son; she knew what a loss men were causing themselves. Through the years she has not changed. Mary is always, thanks be to God, the Refuge of Sinners.

Mary is our mother because she is the mother of Christ; Mary is our mother because of her special association with the work of the redemption; Mary is our mother because the dying Christ solemnly proclaimed it from the cross.

Thus, in the third word from the cross, our Savior not only announced the dignity of Mary but gave her a function to be exercised continually in the future. She is the spiritual mother of all. The mystery of our redemption was foreshadowed even when Mary gave herself up to be the handmaid of the Lord about the age of fifteen saying: "Be it done unto me according to Thy word."

Today no grace comes to us without the cooperation

of Mary. St. Bernard says that "God wills us to obtain all through Mary."

Let us always turn to Mary, as Christ bid us do. He was addressing those words to each one of us when He said: "Behold thy mother." Think of the thousands in hell today who will always regret the greatest mistake of their lives...lost souls repeating forever: "If I had only turned to Mary."

The Fourth Word

"My God, My God, why hast Thou forsaken Me?"

It is nearing three o'clock, the ninth hour. The end is drawing near. Those who know the signs of death have no doubt of it. The two by His side may linger on, but for Christ, the loss of blood since the agony of Gethsemane, the fasting since the evening before, the unrest of that night, the torture of the day, the scourging, and now the crucifixion have utterly exhausted His strength.

And what has our Savior done while hanging there on the cross? He has besought pardon for sinners, He has forgiven the good thief and promised him paradise, He has chosen Mary, His mother, for our mother. And now He begins to feel in the interior of His soul the greatest pains and afflictions, even the agony and pangs of death. Jesus has reached the height of His victory.

Reflection on the ingratitude of men takes strong possession of His mind. He sees the crimes of the wicked and the indifference of the good, the little profit mankind will get from His passion, the sorrows of His blessed Mother. Added to this are His own pains and torments.

Praying to His heavenly Father, foreseeing that His death will be of no avail for many, and now, in the midst of these torments of mind and body, without the least consolation, He cries out: "My God, My God, why hast Thou forsaken Me?"

This is the cry of one abandoned by God. By this cry from the depths of His Heart, Christ is making atonement for those who do abandon God.

He atones for those who have denied God. He atones for those who have known Him, but who live as though they had never heard His name. He atones for those who have lived for the things of this world, giving little or no heed to the next life. The Savior suffers for them now that they may escape the torment of the hereafter, the torment of being abandoned by God.

Think of the many many souls who have been abandoned by God through their own fault because they first abandoned Him. The fallen angels have been abandoned by God forever. Men and women have been abandoned by God because they fell into despair; giving up all hope, hating their own lives they thrust themselves completely away from Him by commiting suicide. And what a sad fate for one of His own apostles, and for all those who have gone the way of Judas.

Because of His human nature, Christ understands human weakness perfectly. He understands human suffering. He Himself suffered all that we could suffer and more. If there is ever a period in our lives when we are tempted to despair, then it is time to recall this fourth word: "My God, why hast Thou forsaken Me?" This is an act of faith, calling on God. It means that the one thing a human heart desires most is not to be forsaken by Him. We need Him and nothing else will satisfy our longing for peace of soul, except God. So if at times we become utterly depressed, lonely, completely discouraged, and crushed so that even prayer seems impossible, even then there is still One to cling to. Jesus knows how I feel. He felt that way Himself.

Meditating on this fourth word we should make some effort to understand the inner feelings of Christ as He hung between heaven and earth, seemingly lost to both. In the garden of Gethsemane, although He had identified Himself with the sinner, Jesus could still say: "My Father." But now, on the cross, it is no longer "My Father" but "My God." Now He knows by experience all that man endures. He is so forsaken in this mystery that God Himself withdraws from Him, and this at the very moment when our Savior gives the greatest proof of His love. And why? That I, a sinner, may never abandon Him. He is my Lord and my Shepherd.

> Who knoweth best, in kindness leadeth me
> In weary ways, where heavy shadows be;
> Out of the sunshine warm and soft and bright,
> Out of the sunshine, into the darkest night.
> I oft would faint with sorrow and affright,
> Only for this, I know He holds my hand.

The Fifth Word

"I thirst!"

Christ came into the world for a definite purpose, to save the world from sin. That is why He has come into your life and mine. And that is why He would love to come into the lives of all.

"Other sheep I have that are not of this fold. Them also I must bring, and they shall hear my voice and there shall be one fold and one Shepherd."

Now nearing the end of His life, the Shepherd calls to the souls of the world, "I thirst!" Though He was suffering intensely from physical thirst, this word signifies also His thirst for souls. He has loved sinners to the very end. From His Sacred Heart comes that pleading voice, "Quench My thirst. Give Me thy soul. I am dying that you may live."

One more suffering is possible. When He said, "I thirst," did He realize what the result would be? He knew perfectly. "Afterwards, Jesus knowing that all things were now accomplished that the Scripture might be fulfilled, said: "I thirst." Now there was a vessel set there full of vinegar. And they, putting a sponge full of vinegar about hyssop, put it to his mouth" (John 19, 28-29).

He did not refuse. He took the bitter vinegar. His lips, swollen and fevered, were seared by the bitter drink. His parched tongue and throat are scalded as the vinegar burned its way through His mouth. Great, wracking coughs convulsed His body, tearing the wounds in His hands and feet wide open again.

The thirst of the crucified is said to be sufficient of itself to cause death. The cruel mockery of Christ's thirst hastened still further His oncoming death. "In my thirst, they gave me vinegar to drink."

Why did our Savior submit to this final act of suffering? Because He is a Savior, He would make atonement during these last few moments for the common sins of gluttony and drunkenness.

From His cross, He sees this world of today, as we see it today, worrying about the specter of atomic destruction, and yet plunging deeper into moral and spiritual destruction. He sees all the effects of the sin of drunkenness: broken families, wives and children beaten, sins of impurity, highway death, thefts, murders. To atone for the sins committed by the slaves of drink, Christ offered His own dying thirst.

It is true that we may have some idea of the physical thirst of Christ upon the cross. But there is no measure for the thirst of Christ for souls. As much as He desired to save all souls from eternal damnation, still that unending procession of souls falling into hell was present to Him on Calvary.

From His cross on Calvary, Christ sees another group. He sees men and women the world over who are willing to appease His thirst for souls. They are willing to leave home, parents, friends, comforts and pleasures in order to work for souls. They understand Christ's loving appeal to their generosity in the words, "I thirst!"

Thus it is that each year groups of religious set sail for the foreign missions where they work and sacrifice themselves unceasingly, "in much patience, in tribulation, in necessities, in labors, in watchings, and fastings, in chastity, in knowledge and long sufferings," happy if they can bring souls to their Creator and Lord.

Though strange sights in the eyes of the world, these missionaries form one of the happiest groups on earth. Their heartfelt joy comes in working through Christ, with Christ, and for Christ. If you should be so favored as to hear the dying plea of Christ for mission-workers, pray for guidance that you may be another to join the crusade to help quench His thirst for love of souls.

Here in the homeland, parents, teachers, doctors, nurses and many others are likewise called upon to assuage the thirst of Christ for souls. Everyone can be an apostle by good example to the "other sheep I have that are not of this fold."

Whatever our occupation may be, Christ's word from the Cross is an appeal to all. During this year may our aim be this: to bring at least one other soul nearer to our loving Shepherd.

The Sixth Word

"It is consummated."

It is the expression of having fulfilled His Father's Will to the very end. What is consummated? The work of Redemption. The Sacrifice is perfect; the work is completed. The seed has been sown.

How quickly those thirty-three years have passed! The happy years of childhood, the voice and touch of His mother, her warmth and gentleness are not forgotten. Then came the work of His hands as a carpenter during the years of His hidden life. Still another phase of life brings hope and gladness...His mission to the world. Beginning with His baptism, and continuing through days of fasting, temptation, labor and prayer, Christ spent His public life doing good to all. How full and active a life giving sight to the blind, cleansing lepers, comforting the poor, teaching and instructing all classes of people. And where does this life of continual labor and suffering lead Him? To the cross. Kindness, mercy and self sacrifice ending in failure with violence, brutality and death! Could it be true?

But let us look a bit closer. Is this real failure? No, indeed, it is the greatest success. The gentleness, the humility, the courage, the generosity, all are consummated. His triumph is at hand. It is victory! A consummation... something that could never be undone...our salvation! "If your sins be as scarlet, they shall be made as white as snow" (Is. 1, 18).

This is the victory of Christ upon the cross. And He is most anxious that we too have a share in His victory. How few there are who finish the work God gave them to do. God wants us to become saints, and perhaps we haven't even begun the task in earnest. But it is never too late. We can take courage from those faithful souls at the foot of the cross. They remain in prayerful silence, Mary His mother, Mary Magdalen, and John, innocence, penitence, and priesthood, the three types of souls ever to be found beneath the cross of Christ.

Now the world about them seems lost in darkness. There are only a few who remain on Calvary and they are motionless. The final moments are slipping by, with each drop of His Precious Blood draining away His life.

Is there some way by which His life could be prolonged? Thanks be to God, there is! Although Christ's physical body is about to die, our Lord foresees the future life of His Mystical Body, the Church. Christ's own life is prolonged in us, the members of that Body. He will continue to live, work and suffer in us. My sufferings then, are truly Christ-sufferings, the two of us suffering in one flesh. St. Paul has proclaimed this truth by saying, "I fill up those things that are wanting in the sufferings of Christ, in my flesh, for His body, which is the Church" (Col. 1, 24).

Does this mean that Christ's sufferings for the salvation of souls were insufficient? No indeed. It means that Christ foresaw the sufferings of St. Paul, your sufferings, my sufferings, all suffering. Of themselves they would have no value, but when united with His sufferings, they become completely transformed into Christ-sufferings ... for the salvation of souls. This is our part in the Mystical Body of Christ; our part in the mystery of the Redemption.

On this subject, Pope Pius XII wrote the following: "Deep mystery this ... that the salvation of many depends on the prayers and voluntary penances which the members of the Mystical Body of Christ offer for this intention, and on the assistance of pastors of souls and the faithful especially of fathers and mothers of families, which they must offer to our Divine Savior as though they were His associates."

Consequently, when God permits us to suffer, He is offering us an active participation in the cross of Christ. It is this truth that should not only give us courage to bear hardships and afflictions which befall us, but to accept them gratefully and even joyfully.

Not to be separated from the cross of Christ means not to be separated from the love of Christ. In the words of St. Paul: "Who then shall separate us from the love of Christ? Shall tribulation or distress, or famine, or nakedness, or danger or persecution or the sword? For I am sure that neither death, nor life, nor angels, nor principalities, nor powers, nor things to come, nor height, nor depth, nor any other creature shall be able to separate us from the love of God, which is in Christ Jesus our Lord" (Rom. 8, 35, 38).

> O living Christ
> Who still dost all
> Our burdens share,
> Come now and dwell
> Within the hearts
> Of all men everywhere!

> —J. Oxenham

The Seventh Word

"Father, into Thy hands I commend my spirit.

His work, His Father's business is finished. We note that Christ begins and ends His agony on the cross with the title, "Father"—"Father forgive them"; "Father into Thy hands I commend my spirit."

JESUS DIES UPON THE CROSS

"And behold the veil of the temple was rent in two from the top even to the bottom, and the earth quaked, and the rocks were rent. And the graves were opened: and the bodies of the saints that slept arose" (Matt. 27,

51-52). Christ's sacred head dropped on His breast; His heart was still. With His final breath He offered Himself to His Father, "Father, into Thy hands I commend my spirit."

It was the darkest hour the world had ever known. God wanted to impress upon the evil doers the tremendous crime they committed. The pride of Jerusalem was crushed; the veil of the temple was rent into two. Those who had shouted in their madness, "If thou be the Son of God, come down from the cross," were now striking their breasts in fear and trembling. "Indeed, this was the Son of God." Why hadn't they said this before? Jesus would not have contradicted the statement. But no, pride is the reason for this terrible deed. The pride of man put Jesus to death. Pride can destroy my soul forever. O, Jesus meek and humble of heart make my heart like unto Thine.

Now the crowd has left Calvary. Let us come close to His mother and our mother. Her love lingers there. Yes, Mary remains. Her soul is wrung in an agony of heartbroken grief as she realizes all the cruel bitterness of this separation from the One Who has been her love and her life. I look up at the Body of Jesus as it hangs there, a pitiful sight, all bloodstained, one mass of cruel wounds. The crown of thorns is crushed down into His head, His eyes no longer seeing, His lips no longer speaking, His ears no longer hearing. And this...all for me...for love of my soul! My crucified Jesus, bless all in their agony today.

We read in Holy Scripture: "One of the soldiers with a spear opened His side, and immediately there came out blood and water," emblems of the Eucharist and

Baptism! In life and in death His Heart is overflowing with graces for repentant sinners.

Devotion to the Sacred Heart of Jesus began with the few who witnessed His sacrifice to the very end. Now the last drop of His Precious Blood has trickled down His side. All the saints in heaven are saints because of His Precious Blood. We are looking at the Sacred Heart of Jesus, the font of all sanctity.

How wonderful that He has not left us orphans to look back on this closing scene of His life without hope for the future.

No, we are not left without His loving care. As children in need of His Life, He has given to us the Holy Sacrifice of the Mass. Through the consecrated hands of the priest, our Savior continues to offer Himself to the Father. He begs us to offer ourselves, body and soul, in union with His own oblation. "Father into Thy hands I commend my spirit."

A little prayer to welcome our Lord at Mass:

> Come, dear Jesus, on this morn,
> Within my heart again be born,
> Make me feel throughout the day,
> That You really wish to stay
> Within my soul to light and cheer
> By Your Presence ever near.
> Unite me with Your Mother too
> In all that I may say and do.
> Make my heart an altar shrine,
> Of sacrifice and Love Divine!
> Then only heaven will surpass
> The beauty of this morning's Mass.

—By a missionary.

THE
FOURTH
WEEK

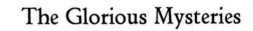

The Glorious Mysteries

The Resurrection

First Glorious Mystery

This is the Fourth Week of the *Spiritual Exercises,* a period of spiritual joy and consolation. We have followed our Blessed Lord through combat to victory. The Fourth Week likewise appeals to our generosity, because He who has given all should not have less than all in return.

The scene:

I shall visualize the resurrection of our Lord and His visit to His mother (Matt. 28, 1-9).

The petition:

I shall ask for the "grace to be glad and rejoice intensely for the great joy of Christ our Lord."

THE RESURRECTION

"Let us rejoice, O my beloved.
Let us go forth to see ourselves in Thy Beauty."

228 / THE SHEPHERD OF MY SOUL

The events leading up to the Resurrection give to this mystery its undeniable proof. Late Good Friday afternoon, Joseph and Nicodemus took down the body of Christ and anointed it. Our Lord had no grave of His own; He was placed in the sepulchre belonging to Joseph of Arimathea. The stone was rolled over the entrance and Mary, John and the holy women returned to Jerusalem. Mindful of Christ's prophecy, the priests asked Pilate to have a guard placed at the tomb. He told them to use their own guards and they did...another proof of the resurrection.

"Very early in the morning" the Scripture tells us, Christ arose from the dead. By His almighty power, He passed through the sealed stone raised above the tomb in His beautiful glorified body. The wounds remain but from them shines a bright light; they are now the five glorious wounds. So much for the body of Christ. But what of His soul?

The soul of our Savior brought the glad tidings to those in Limbo. For thousands of years, Adam and Eve, the patriarchs and prophets had been waiting for the promised Messiah. And during the lifetime of our Lord, the holy innocents, Anna, Simeon and dear St. Joseph. John the Baptist brought the news that he had seen the Lamb of God. The good thief heard Him say: "This day thou shalt be with Me in paradise." What a glorious reunion it was for all those souls to be with their King!

OUR LORD APPEARS TO HIS MOTHER

St. Ignatius says: "First He appeared to the Virgin Mary, which though not told in the Scripture, is included in the words that He appeared to many." St. Teresa writes:

"He said to me that when He rose again, He showed Himself to our Lady, because she was in great trouble; for sorrow had so pierced her soul that she did not even recover herself at once in order to have the fruition of that joy. By this I saw how different was my piercing. But what must that of the Virgin have been. He remained long with her then, because it was necessary to console her." Christ consoles His Mother with the assurance of possessing Him for eternity. So likewise does He console us. With holy Job we can say: "But as for me, I know that my Vindicator lives...Whom I myself shall see, and not another, and from my flesh I shall see God" (Job 19, 25-26).

This gives us a picture of the Mother of Sorrows and makes us understand a little how deeply her pure soul had been pierced. Though she had probably spent Saturday in consoling others, though she knew that His sufferings were all over and that He would rise again, though she was waiting for Him and now seeing Him in all His wondrous beauty, yet the joy could not at first enter her broken heart, because the cross was still so vivid, the nails, the thorns. But when joy did enter her soul it was in proportion to the sorrow. "Your sorrow shall be turned into joy."

Now Mary beholds more vividly her God. And she rejoices that He is her own Son. And now there passes before her mind His life, the Incarnation, the happy months of waiting for His birth, the Nativity, the coming of the shepherds, the visit of the Magi, the little home at Nazareth. How quickly did those years seem to pass by. And then came His first miracle, at the wedding feast in Cana, His care for the sick and poor...and finally His dying words, when He gave His mother to be our mother. Yes, because of my Son, says Mary to herself, "All generations shall call me blessed." We also rejoice in the happiness of our blessed Mother.

Now I shall look once again at these two, Jesus and Mary. How they have changed my heart, the Sacred Heart of Jesus and the Immaculate Heart of Mary. They alone can change the world.

She gazes at Him again, never realizing before, the beauty that is His. This was her Risen Savior. Mary adores His Sacred Heart. The devotion of the Sacred Heart has begun. And Jesus looks at the Immaculate Heart of Mary. It was the living image of His own, beautiful, pure and filled with grace. He looks into her heart and He looks into her future. She will be the mother of His Church.

He sees the Immaculate Heart of Mary, open as a flood-gate through which all the graces of His heart would flow into the heart of His future popes, bishops, priests, brothers, nuns and all those faithful souls, members of the Apostleship of Prayer, the Sodality, the Legion of Mary, to all the children of Mary, children of Her Immaculate Heart. A vision of the City of God. "Let us rejoice, O my Beloved. Let us go forth to see ourselves in Thy Beauty" (words of St. John of the Cross).

THEIR JOY AND OUR JOY

Can we imagine what the resurrection meant to Mary Magdalene? Remember, her heart had been nailed to the cross of Christ. If she had loved much before, her love was even greater now. She came to the tomb seeking Christ. The huge stone barring the sepulchre had been rolled aside. Here I must realize God's power to put aside any obstacle in my life that would keep me from Him. Finding Him gone did not deter Mary nor diminish her eagerness to find where they had taken Him. At the moment He *seemed* lost He was actually present. In my own prayers, is it not the same? And then Magdalene heard the voice she had learned to love: "Mary." I will try to appreciate this little scene because it is a perfect picture of conquest...divine love conquering human love, or rather elevating it to the supernatural level.

Let us look at Peter for a moment. Undoubtedly he must have felt that he did not deserve to see Jesus very soon. Meanwhile, Peter had learned his lesson. Yes, he had repented from the depths of his heart. We shall see him again in a coming meditation. To Mary Magdalene and to all the apostles, the resurrection meant confirmation in faith, great peace of soul, and intense spiritual joy.

What does the resurrection mean to us? Better still, just what does it mean to me personally? St. Paul has answered the question conclusively: "If Christ be not risen again, then is our preaching vain, and your faith is also vain." Consequently the truth of the resurrection is the foundation of our faith. He died for me personally; He rose from the dead for me personally. Consequently, I rejoice from the bottom of my heart for the One who conquered death itself that I might live. Likewise I rejoice with His own mother and friends who followed Him through the Passion to victory. I rejoice with the saints who have served Him, the martyrs who have sacrificed their lives to the present day, who like Fr. Pro, S.J., have raised their voices in lasting praise: "Long live Christ the King."

It is the resurrection of Christ that has won the victory for all the faithful, and because of His resurrection there is hope for mine. After the cross the crown. After death to a life of sin comes the courage for a life of grace, of generosity and union with Christ, so that I also may say with St. Paul: "I live now, no not I but Christ liveth in me" (Gal. 11, 20).

He lives in each one of us. Surely we are encouraged likewise to go on now to our own spiritual resurrection for which we have prepared. "Just as Christ has risen from the dead through the glory of the Father, so we also may walk in newness of life" (Rom. 6, 4). It is this "newness of life" that our Holy Father the Pope bids us esteem and enjoy.

THE LORD IS RISEN

The greatest joy the world could hope for was expressed by an angel at the sepulchre: "You seek Jesus of Nazareth who was crucified. He is risen...!" (Mark 16, 6).

Easter is the greatest feast of the year. Our Risen Lord wishes to bring gladness and peace to all. Indeed, He wishes all to recognize Him as the Redeemer of mankind. We listen to the words of Pope Paul spoken recently, "Nothing is more dear to Our Lady than this recognition by men of her Son, Who is the Friend, the King and Redeemer of souls. Let us invoke Him above all as the King of Peace, of that peace for which the world has all the greater need, the more it seems unable to achieve it."

The beauty of Easter is expressed in these lines:

In spirit we have walked the path

Where Jesus dragged His cross,
And watched in anguish on the hill
Where earth first knew its loss.
Now spring returns and tulips bloom
And Easter lilies grow,
For Resurrection is His gift
Which all God's children know.

My Good Shepherd has brought me to this happy moment, for I realize better Who He is and what I am. Dear Jesus, lead me forward by Your loving care today. Let Yourself in me meet Yourself in my neighbor, and through my little prayers may others also come to know Yourself so that there may be more and more happiness here and hereafter.

Christ Appears on the Shore of Tiberias

Up to the time of His Passion, our Lord had instructed the apostles in the fundamentals of the Church, His Kingdom upon earth. But the apostles were still quite worldly-minded and did not grasp all that He wished to convey to them, nor would they until the coming of the Holy Ghost at Pentecost. Jesus, therefore, in the interval between the Resurrection and the Ascension frequently came and conversed with them. He appeared to the group in Jerusalem twice within the eight days after Easter, once on Easter itself, and once on the Octave. The eighth appearance was in Galilee on the shore of Lake Tiberias.

The scene:

> I shall endeavor to witness this scene by the lake, seeing the apostles and Christ comforting them (John 21, 1-17).

The petition:

> I will ask for the grace to appreciate the companionship of Christ in my life.

THE FISHERMAN

"I go afishing"...it is Peter, the chief fisherman who has sounded the call to work. The apostles respond: "We also come with thee." And we shall say the same. These men were the best of fishermen, and yet we are told that they labored all night and caught nothing. Not one fish. If we have ever gone fishing for a few hours and caught nothing, we know that it is difficult enough. These men were out on the lake all night. Tired, sleepy, hungry, and nothing to show the result of their labor. Regarding the acquiring of virtue even of a single virtue, our own lives seem the same. The same empty boat, the same empty heart. The lesson is this: in God's service to try is to succeed. The result is not always visible. God has not asked for success, nor has He promised it, but He asks for our best, our effort. He has gained the victory and our own little failures or successes do not count for much either way, but our efforts do count, because that is the part that God sees, as well as the results of our labors. Our Lord knew that the apostles had caught nothing, but had labored much. Perhaps they had counted too much on their own skill.

OUR LORD APPEARS ON THE SHORE

"When the morning was come, Jesus stood on the shore, yet the disciples knew not that it was Jesus." He has been there all the time, but like the apostles, we do not recognize Him in our failures. They are sent to us by God.

Jesus stood on the shore...now He calls to them. "Have you anything to eat?" They answered Him: "No." They acknowledge their failure at once. Have we always succeeded? No. Then, let us imitate the example of the apostles and not be surprised at our faults and failures. Then our Lord said to them: "Cast the net on the right side of the boat." What happened? "They were not able to draw in the net for the multitude of fishes." The victory is His, not theirs, nor ours.

Then the disciple whom Jesus loved, said to Peter: "It is the Lord." Our own little successes will never hurt us, if we say at once: "It is the Lord. To Him be the praise and glory."

The less we think we are, the more good we do. It was only when the apostles had labored all the night and taken nothing that our Lord filled the boat with the miraculous draught of fishes. God's instruments for good in the world are chiefly the humble. Reducing themselves to zero, they leave room for infinity, whereas those who think themselves all important are often left helpless by God.

CHRIST PREPARES THE FOOD

"As soon as they had come to land, they saw hot coals lying, and a fish laid thereon and bread." He knew that they were tired and hungry and He prepared everything for them.

"Bring of the fishes which you have now caught," He says. Why this order? He could have used other fish besides the ones they had caught. But the fish they had caught would make them feel their share in the victory of Christ. The apostles, full of love and reverence look at their Master, and while they are hardly able to withdraw their eyes from Him for a single instant, they dare not speak a word. Jesus looks at them silently. His Sacred Heart is overflowing with love for His disciples. It is a silent scene but O how infinitely expressive. It is an image of our own morning Banquet; even now He stands at our altars and prepares there a heavenly meal for us. We approach the Holy Table and we receive the Lamb of God in silence and love. We hear Him asking us the question He put to Peter: "Lovest thou Me?"

Peter replied with humility this time, not with the over-confidence of the supper room, when he promised to be faithful and failed. "Lord, Thou knowest that I love Thee."

Let us listen again to those beautiful words Christ addresses to our souls: "Lovest thou Me?" Love is the only condition of the apostolate. The apostle must love Christ, and for the sake of Christ he must love men and be ready to sacrifice his life for them.

Only when Peter had avowed his love was he made the first Vicar of Christ upon earth. "Feed My lambs; feed My sheep." They are all *His* lambs and *His* sheep. He is the Good Shepherd and He wants everybody old and young, to receive the food of their souls. As one of His sheep, I will thank my Good Shepherd now for the many times He has come to my soul.

THE GREAT COMMISSION

We render thanks unto Thee, O Christ our God, who of Thy goodness hast bestowed upon us this Food for the sanctification of our lives; keep us through It holy and without blame under Thy divine protection. Feed us in the pastures of Thy holy and good pleasure, that being strengthened against all the snares of the devil, we may be deemed worthy to hear Thy holy voice, and follow Thee, the one victorious and true Shepherd, and to receive from Thee that place which has been prepared for us in the Kingdom of heaven.

For Thou, O our God and Lord and Savior Jesus Christ, art blessed with the Father and the Holy Spirit, now and forever, world without end. Amen.

The apparitions of our Lord are closely related. Prior to the appearance on Lake Tiberias we are told by St. Matthew (Ch. 28) that "Eleven disciples went into Galilee, to the mountain where Jesus had directed them to go. And Jesus coming spoke to them saying: 'All power is given to Me in heaven and on earth. Go therefore, and teach all nations: baptizing them in the name of the Father, and of the Son, and of the Holy Spirit. Teaching them to observe all things whatsoever I have commanded you: and behold I am with you all days even to the consumation of the world.'"

"Go ... teaching...." When God commands us to teach, He cannot be indifferent as to whether His message is heard, understood, accepted. God's plan is built upon authority and demands obedience. He Who is Truth—commands us to believe truth—"*all* that I have commanded you." Jesus is still with us all days! "Behold I am with you all days even to the consummation of the world."

This Divine promise is the very heart of our spiritual life: it is a vital organic union which binds Head and members into one living body—the Mystical Body of Christ. He is closely united to us as our Good Shepherd, leading us, protecting us—toward the fountain of living water, the fountain of Life, the Bread of Life!

The Ascension

Second Glorious Mystery

We began our series of meditations in the company of Jesus. We have listened to His doctrine; we have seen in Him the living example of all that He taught. In this last scene of His earthly life, let us join the little flock as they walk for the last time with their beloved Master.

The scene:

To witness the Good Shepherd with His faithful flock on the summit of the mountain (Acts 1, 1-12).

The petition:

I will ask for the grace to ascend with Jesus to a life of union with Him.

HIS DEPARTING MESSAGE

Jesus led His apostles in the direction of Bethany, to The Mount of Olives. He desired that His glorious ascension should take place in the vicinity of the garden where His passion had begun, to impress once more on the apostles that "the Son of Man shall be betrayed into the hands of men and they shall kill Him and after He is killed He shall rise again on the third day."

He commands them not to depart from Jerusalem. Do not leave the City of Peace, but wait here until the coming of the Holy Spirit. See how our Lord was planning ahead for their own good. The apostles did not fully understand the great blessings which lay in store for them; consequently, to the very last our Lord wished them to obey. Christ, the Good Shepherd, knew what was best for them, although the apostles may have wanted to go elsewhere for fear of the Jews.

The apostles were told to wait until the coming of the Holy Spirit. We are living in a world that wants everything in a hurry. But, regarding the good of our souls, God knows the best time and place to impart His grace. So if my prayer is not answered immediately, I must realize that God knows what is best for me, now and in the future.

Our Lord told them: "You shall be witnesses unto Me." I want you to be one of my witnesses, one of my representatives on earth. I want you henceforth to be impressed with the idea that you are a representative of your King. The world does not know the Master, but it knows the servants, and I want it to know the Master through the servants. Be so penetrated with my spirit that you will be recognized as one of My disciples. You have promised to follow Me; be true to your resolution.

THE ASCENSION

Present in spirit on Mount Olivet on that memorable day, moving here and there among the assembled crowd, I observe the persons, listen to their conversation, note their conduct. These are all the special loved ones of Jesus. The air is bristling with expectation and mystery. We can imagine the disciples each pressing to be as near to Jesus as possible, but giving reverent preference to His Blessed Mother. Once more a last embrace, Oh, how tenderly a last farewell to His beloved Mother and friends.

"And when He had said these things, lifting up His hands He blessed them, and whilst He blessed them, He departed from them and was carried up to heaven, and a cloud received Him out of their sight."

He is gone; gone back to His Father and to my Father, to His God and to my God. How near heaven seems now to earth. Everyone stood there, His mother included, gazing heavenward, or homeward, we might say, until two angels told them to return to Jerusalem to await the coming of the Holy Spirit.

What other reasons has Christ given before leaving them? "I go to prepare a place for you." He promised that when our part of the battle is over, we will share in the victory with Him. I want you to enjoy My company forever. Although you shall not see Me in the future, I will always be present in the Holy Sacrament of the Altar.

THE APOSTLES RETURN TO JERUSALEM

We are told that the apostles "went back into Jerusalem with great joy, praising and blessing God." So may I. Sadness, trouble and difficulties may await me, but I know that these need not interfere with my joy.

Let us look for a moment to our Blessed Mother. Even after the others had turned and gone back to

Jerusalem, she stood there on the Mount of Olives, looking up toward the brilliant glory of the cloud, the beautiful cloud that had just enveloped her Son. Perhaps she thought she too should be going toward the city. An angel had come to send the apostles back to Jerusalem, but he had said "Ye men of Galilee" as if he did not want to send her away from the mountain, as if he understood her desire to linger there.

Almost involuntarily she raised her eyes. The cloud had disappeared. Our Lord was with His Father. And He had entrusted the world to her and to the apostles. Mary laid her firm hand more trustingly on the arm of John. John smiled eagerly and said just one word: "Mother." That was it. She was a mother. Our Lord had said: "Behold thy mother," and in doing so He had given her not a name but an office, a very responsible office in the world, to mother His brothers and sisters and to guard His infant Church.

"Come," she said softly. Then, slowly and with deep meaning, she added: "How much we have to do. How much of His work we have left to us."

The same may be said of ourselves. How much of His work is left for us to do. I know that God wishes me to become a saint, and sometimes I wonder if I have made any progress at all. In this meditation I have seen the great solicitude of my Good Shepherd. He promised to send the Holy Spirit upon the apostles and now I turn to Him in sincere thanksgiving, not only for that first Pentecost, but for all the wonderful gifts of the Holy spirit to my soul, unworthy though I am. In conclusion—the "Hail Holy Queen."

The Descent of the Holy Spirit

Third Glorious Mystery

In this meditation we see the former promise of Christ fulfilled with the coming of the Paraclete, the Comforter. This descent of the Holy Spirit was to confirm the apostles in their faith and to strengthen them with divine gifts of grace. On this great day the body of the Church received its spirit. And moreover, Mary by her presence and through the Holy Spirit, gave to this newly formed Church of her Divine Son, the blessing of her motherhood.

The scene:

> I shall endeavor to be present at this momentous event in company with the apostles and their queen (Acts 11, 1-6).

The petition:

> Will be to ask the Holy Spirit for a greater appreciation of His spiritual gifts.

THE PREPARATION

The apostles, as we have seen, were uneducated fishermen. It is true that they had learned a great deal from their Master, but they were not leaders of men. Only recently they had witnessed His ascension into heaven. Now they were even more convinced of His power and their own weakness. They realized what a privilege it had been to know and love Him. We are told by St. Luke, "And they adoring went back into Jerusalem with great joy." The Good Shepherd directed their footsteps, although humanly speaking, the return to Jerusalem at this time, might well have meant their death. They needed greater courage and what shall I say of my own soul? What are my desires?

"My son," says the author of the *Imitation of Christ*, "I know thy desires, I have often heard thy frequent sighs. Thou wouldst enjoy the glory of the children of God. Thou wouldst be pleased to be now at thy eternal home, and in thy heavenly country, abounding with joy; but that hour is not yet come; for this is yet another time, a time of war, of labor and of trouble. Take courage, therefore, and be valiant, as well in doing as in suffering things repugnant to nature. Let this be your wish: That whether in life or in death God may be glorified in you" (Chap. 3, 49).

The apostles prior to Pentecost were men of good will and desire, but with uncertain plans for the future. God directed them to the first closed retreat. Cut off from the turmoil of the world and with the quiet of solitude and prayer they were able to prepare their souls. Mary, the beautiful example of humility and prayer could kneel with them. What did her supplications mean for these men of destiny? How grateful they were to the mother of God. He wanted them to perform a particular work and Mary would lead them. The same may be said for each one of us. What does God want me to do? Do I realize how important it is to pray, consult, and listen to God in time of prayer and retreat?

THE DESCENT OF THE HOLY SPIRIT

The day and hour chosen by God had arrived. It was the fiftieth day after the resurrection of our Lord.

Now I shall try to imagine this scene as it is related in the Gospel of St. Luke: "And when the days of the Pentecost were accomplished, they were all together in one place. And suddenly there came a sound from heaven, as of a mighty wind coming, and it filled the whole house where they were sitting. And there appeared to them parted tongues as it were of fire, and it sat upon every one of them. And they were all filled with the Holy Spirit, and they began to speak with divers tongues, according as the Holy Spirit gave them to speak" (Acts 11, 1-4).

Regarding the parted tongues of fire, the text reads, "as it were of fire," to signify that it was not actual fire, but a supernatural fire. This spiritual fire assumed the form of tongues to signify that it came from God endowing the apostles to preach the divine doctrine. St. Bonaventure speaks as follows, "The Holy Spirit is a fire that inflames the affections, enlightens the understanding, kindles the will."

St. Paul gives this description, "Our God is a consuming fire" (Heb. 12, 29). Fire consumes all corrupt matter, it purifies, it refines gold separating it from the dross. Such is the spiritual action of the Holy Spirit upon the soul, namely, cleansing, purifying, and assisting the soul to discern good from apparent good or evil.

Returning to the scene, no greater change in spirit has ever been recorded, than this supernatural change in the apostles. They were no longer selfish and worldly minded, but were imbued with love and zeal for the salvation of their fellowmen. Now they had but one hope, one love, one mission: Christ. Do I fully realize as a Christian that I have this same sacred mission? Am I like the apostles, another Christ-bearer, another Christopher? Do I appreciate the One I bear to the extent of helping others to know and love Him also? In my daily relationship with men, women, and children, do I want the Christ in me to meet and love the Christ in them? If such is my sincere ambition and I feel the need of help, then I should turn often to the Holy Spirit and pray: Come Holy Spirit and enkindle in my heart the spirit of Thy Divine Love.

THE MISSION

Following the descent of the Holy Spirit, the apostles did not delay their mission. They began preaching immediately to the utter amazement of the diverse nationalities present in Jerusalem. Each group understood the message in their own tongue. "And they were all amazed and wondered saying: Behold, are not these that speak Galileans?" (Acts 11, 7). Their preaching bore fruit at once; the Church they established was founded on the charity of Christ. Since the apostles were told to "teach all nations..." it is perfectly clear that God desires all men to hear and understand His doctrine of eternal salvation.

How dear to the Heart of Christ is this mission of spreading the truth! There are many people today who sincerely desire to learn about the Catholic faith, but there are so few to teach them. This work of the lay apostolate is most dear to the heart of our present Pope Paul VI.

Why is it that only a few are willing to teach others? What is lacking? Zeal! The first lesson in divine zeal is this: before we can do good to others, we must first possess Christ in our own lives. The Good Shepherd has told us clearly that we must abide in Him in order to bear fruit.

First, I must have zeal for my own soul. Bringing Him to others means good example on my part; it means being a Christ-bearer. What is there in the world to compare with Christ-like kindness? Haven't I benefitted from the good example and kindness of others? Does this little reflection spark a bit of zeal in my heart to become with and for Christ...an apostle of kindness?

If so, I shall pray with St. Francis of Assisi:

> "Lord, make me an instrument of thy peace.
> Where there is hatred let me sow love;
> where there is injury, pardon; where there
> is doubt, faith; where there is despair, hope;
> where there is darkness, light; where there
> is sadness, joy.
> O, Divine Master, grant that I may not so much
> seek to be consoled as to console; to be
> understood as to understand; to be loved as
> to love; for it is by giving that we receive;
> it is by pardoning that we are pardoned; and
> it is by dying that we are born to eternal
> life." Amen.

To become an instrument of God's peace as St. Francis and other saints were, I will turn to the Holy Spirit and say this little prayer:

> "O Holy Spirit, Soul of my soul, I adore Thee.
> Strengthen, guide, enlighten and console me,
> and tell me what I ought to do, and command
> me to do it. I promise to be submissive in all
> Thou shalt ask of me, and I promise to accept
> all that Thou permittest to happen to me. Only
> show me what is Thy will." Amen.

The Assumption of the Blessed Mother

Fourth Glorious Mystery

In this mystery we contemplate the final event in the life of Mary on earth. She gave her Son His human life, and He, being God, gives her in return the glorious life of Immortality. As an angel took part in the Incarnation, we may well believe an angel took part in Mary's glorious assumption into heaven. We, too rejoice in this recently defined dogma of our faith, for Mary is truly our heavenly mother.

The scene:

Here I will endeavor to imagine Mary borne heavenward, leaving an empty grave as a proof of her Assumption.

The petition:

I will ask for the grace to live a pure life, so that my body and soul may be united with God forever.

THE DEATH OF MARY

Because her Son had died, Mary too must pass through the portals of death. The hour came when she simply closed her eyes with heartfelt confidence that she would soon behold the beauty of her Son. She had in all probability witnessed the risen glory of her Son soon after the resurrection, but not surrounded by the court of heaven. This was to be her reward now for such a perfect life of praise, reverence and service. She had been a perfect mother to Jesus, and a perfect mother to His Church upon earth. Yes, she had been the perfect model for all virgins and mothers, through all generations. If virgins and mothers today took Mary as a closer model, wouldn't the world be far different, far happier?

We can't expect a perfect world or a near perfect world here below, "mourning and weeping in this valley of tears." But we can expect through fidelity to grace that Mary will "after this our exile, show unto us the blessed fruit of her womb, Jesus."

Again, I shall glance upon Mary at her moment of death. Was she alone? If they knew that she was dying, certainly the apostles would have been there to the very end. How reverently they would have carried her to the grave. She had been their Queen, and looking on her for the last time upon earth, they must have realized to the full this truth: Heaven is home, the earth a mere place of exile, suffering and death. And what might be written over her little grave? So many beautiful titles could be chosen, but one surpasses them all: The Mother of God.

HER GLORIOUS ASSUMPTION

Here we are at loss for words in trying to describe another beautiful mystery. But we read in Holy Scripture a text fully verified in Mary's glorious assumption. Surely it could be said of Mary that "she cometh up from the desert, flowing with delights, leaning upon her beloved" (Cant. 8, 5). Would not her beloved Son arise to come and greet His own Mother? Could He welcome her except with His own Divine Love. Here no words are necessary. Such love is beyond words. Only love is present, but to such a perfect degree that heaven itself reaches a new climax of joy, with the presence of King and Queen together. One and all rejoice with their heavenly Queen, the angels, martyrs, virgins and the entire court of heaven. Whatever splendor could be imagined for an earthly queen on her day of coronation would not begin to touch the beauty of Mary on this glorious occasion of her Assumption into heaven.

Now I must realize that God wishes me also to have a share in this wonderful mystery. He wants me to honor this mystery while saying the rosary. Above all, He wants me to look upward, above this vale of tears to the great reward of heaven, promised to a child of Mary.

MARY, THE CAUSE OF OUR JOY

Mary is looking down upon me now. My heavenly mother loves me so much because I bear within my soul the very image of Her Divine Son. As a loving mother, she never wants me to forget my final goal: life everlasting!

What do we see about us? How pathetically, how frantically do people cling to this present mortal life. We are prone to treasure it above all riches and pleasures. To preserve, to defend it, we are ready to hazard all else. But what is this mortal life compared with the *true* life which God has prepared for those who love Him? "Eye hath not seen, nor ear heard nor has it entered into the heart of man, what things God has prepared for those who love Him" (1 Cor. 2, 9). So Eternal Wisdom tells us through the voice of St. Paul.

It is a real blessing to evaluate this present life for what it really is. Hasn't it seemed to pass very quickly so far? Indeed it is but a fleeting moment in God's eternal plan. "For our present light affliction, which is for the *moment,* prepares us for an eternal weight of glory that is beyond all measure" (2 Cor. 4, 17). Thousands of years ago God promised to Abraham: "I am thy reward exceeding great" (Gen. 15, 1). And this is the same promise that He makes to me.

What is the trouble with many of us. We are too busy —like Martha—about many things so that we rarely come to the feet of Jesus to ponder the more important things of life. We all need the example of Mary, who "kept all these things pondering them in her heart."

In conclusion, I will turn to my heavenly mother, and ask for the grace of purity of mind and body, thereby becoming through her intercession a less unworthy child of God. Conclude with the "Hail Mary."

Heaven

In the meditation on the "Kingdom of Christ," our Lord urged us to share His labors and sufferings by the consideration of the part we would eventually have in His glory. The time has come to cheer us on and to arouse us to valor and generosity in life's struggle by this meditation on heaven.

The scene:

> I will endeavor to behold Jesus, my King, seated on His throne at the right side of the Father and crowned with glory and majesty.

The petition:

I will ask for an ardent desire of heaven, and the grace to so live my life as to receive this reward.

THE JOY OF HEAVEN

In heaven we shall be free of all ills of body and soul. This earth is the land of exile, the land of miseries. It is an abode of pain and affliction. To suffer and die, such is life on earth. But in heaven these words are unknown. St. Ignatius thought of heaven frequently. "How sordid is the world, when I gaze into the heavens." The happiness and joy that we do experience from time to time is only a prelude to the eternal happiness of heaven.

Various individuals have expressed themselves on this subject. A dear old Irish lady after a hard day's work expressed her thoughts in these few words, "O, I wish I was up in heaven sitting down!" In heaven there will be no noise and there will be no dust. There will be no worries of any kind. All will be tranquil and peaceful. Not a single unkind thought could exist in heaven. The soul is perfectly happy and knows that this joy is to last forever.

Have the saints experienced a foretaste of this joy? Let us imagine for a moment two great saints sitting side by side, mother and son, in their little home at Ostia. It is evening and they are looking up to the heavens, conversing on the greatness and beauty of God. "When suddenly," we are told from the writings of St. Augustine, "the heavens opened for a moment." Whatever St. Augustine and St. Monica beheld in vision we do not know. But it would seem that momentarily God rewarded them, giving to them as He did to St. Paul, a foretaste of the joy of heaven.

OUR LORD SPEAKS OF HEAVEN

Heaven was the principal theme of His many hours of preaching to the people. By way of comparison, Christ likened the kingdom of heaven to a net cast into the sea, a treasure hidden in a field, a pearl of great price, and a marriage feast.

Let us picture Him for a moment on the mountain top speaking to the people. What is He doing? With His arms outstretched, He is exhorting souls to the future life of the blessed in heaven.

Listen to the voice of Christ as He speaks with a tone of kindness and authority. "Blessed are the poor in spirit ... Blessed are they that mourn ... Blessed are the clean of heart ... Blessed are those who suffer persecution." Yes, in His own gentle way He promised an eternal blessing to the poor in spirit, the meek, the chaste, those who hunger and thirst after divine justice, the persecuted and the peacemakers. And now, where is that vast army of the faithful since the time of Christ? They are enjoying the reward of the blessed in heaven; they have led the way for each of us.

Each group is so aptly represented in that beautiful array of faithful souls: the poor in spirit by St. Francis of Assisi, the meek by St. Alphonsus, the mourners or penitents by St. Mary Magdalene and St. Peter Damien, the seekers of divine justice by St. Benedict and St. Charles Borromeo, the merciful by St. John of God, the pure of heart by St. Theresa and St. Aloysius.

All of these, and countless other saints and martyrs

lived on the same earth that we do. They had many of the same trials and sufferings as we do. God's grace was never wanting in their lives; it will not be wanting in our own. As God called others who became saints, so does He call us to sanctity. The call to heaven is the same for all. It is an upward call.

HEAVEN IS AN UPWARD CALL

On earth many of the most wonderful and beautiful things are above us. The sun rises above us; the beautiful blue sky is above us. In the evening, the starlit heavens form a canopy over our heads. From the trees, to the hills, to the mountains, God has ever been directing our gaze upwards. Like little children who look upwards to their fathers and mothers, God the Father of all has deigned to have us raise our eyes above...heavenward.

But God has called us to do more than lift our eyes toward heaven. He has called us to lift our hearts to heaven. *"Sursum corda!"*, Lift up your hearts! These words are spoken during every Mass. They bid us seek the things that are above. "Therefore, if you be risen with Christ, seek the things that are above; where Christ is sitting at the right hand of God. Mind the things that are above, not the things that are upon the earth" (Col. 3, 1-2).

The call of Christ is not loud and forceful but gentle and appealing. The reason why we do not hear His voice oftener than we do is because we fail to listen attentively. Sometimes even for religious the call seems far away. It seems to be coming in our direction, but not exactly to be so near as to be a continual and urgent sound knocking at the door of our hearts. And yet it is true, the persistent call of Christ to perfection, to sanctity. The question is, are we ready to follow His call?

If so, we are much the same as a person about to climb a steep mountain, or rather like one who has progressed some distance and finds the going more difficult. Each step forward in the direction of God is one step further away from self. Each step calls for the practice of virtue. We thank God for the wonderful example of the saints who have followed in the footsteps of Christ.

He is the Leader for all who desire to follow Him. Being true man as well as true God, He possessed our human nature and as such was subject to weariness, hunger and thirst. Moreover, He permitted Himself to be tempted by the devil. And we know the outcome of His temptations. The answer of Christ given to the devil is the same that we must give. "Begone, Satan; for it is written: The Lord thy God shalt thou adore, and Him only shalt thou serve" (Matt. 4, 10).

So often, we are told, Christ lifted His eyes toward heaven, to His Father. In this manner He taught us to pray, "Our Father Who art in heaven...." In meditating on the public life of our Lord, we witnessed Him going from place to place teaching the people everywhere about the kingdom of heaven until the closing days of His life on earth. We saw Him climb the hill of Calvary slowly and painfully with the crushing burden of the cross. He foresaw that His sacrifice would lift us from earth to heaven.

And so through the ages, the followers of Christ, the saints have not only looked upward, but they have struggled upward. The saints of today do the same. Steadily they climb away from evil, away from the devil, and their lower nature, upward, toward their higher nature, toward the angels, toward Mary, toward Christ, toward the Adorable Trinity. Heaven forever! Conclude with the "Our Father."

The Coronation of the Blessed Mother

Fifth Glorious Mystery

As the attention of the world has been directed at various times in history to the coronation of a queen, attention in this meditation is also focused on a queen, but one that has been elevated above the honor and glory of the world to reign forever in the glorious realm of the blessed. Mary is a Queen. She is God's own choice for the angels and saints to honor as the Mother of Christ the King, and the Queen of heaven.

The scene:

To imagine myself in the presence of Mary the most beautiful Queen.

The petition:

To ask for the grace to so live now, as to merit the joy of the blessed in heaven.

HAIL MARY, FULL OF GRACE

This is the reason why Mary is Queen. She received and now enjoys God's grace to the full. There were those on earth who believed in Mary's wonderful gifts of grace: St. Joseph, St. Simeon, St. Elizabeth, St. John the Baptist, the Apostles and others. She was queen on earth before she became queen of heaven. And this is precisely what every one of us should realize. Mary must be my Queen now while on earth if I wish to enjoy her presence forever in heaven.

There is nothing that Mary desires more than my cooperation with Divine grace as the essential means of salvation and sanctification. She is the mother of grace; I am her child. Am I doing my duty as a faithful child of so dear a mother? What a beautiful example of her love do many of the fifteen mysteries of the rosary reveal. Am I devoted to the rosary and do I try to lead the little ones nearer to Mary through the family rosary?

I should never fail to employ this means of obtaining grace for my own and the salvation of other souls. This is an important part of the message of Fatima: Pray the rosary!

HAIL HOLY QUEEN!

What words could possibly express the joy of heaven? At times we may glimpse a little foretaste of heaven through the beauty and harmony of nature. There is harmony of color in a beautiful sunset, there is harmony of sound in a beautiful symphony. But what must the harmony and beauty of heaven be? If there is so much beauty in the natural, what must the supernatural be? Even with everything the universe may offer, still, "Eye hath not seen, nor ear heard, nor hath it entered into the heart of man what things God hath prepared for them that love Him" (1 Cor. 2, 9).

Is heaven to be mine? Yes, if I ask my heavenly

mother for the grace I need now, the grace to be faithful in keeping all the Commandments and in following a plan of life based on the observance of the beatitudes.

This Fifth Glorious Mystery teaches me that I am preparing my soul for heaven. What a consolation it is to realize that even now my mother is heaven's Queen!

> Whene're I doubt if one so base as I,
> Shall share with heavenly choirs,
> Their joys serene,
> This thought brings solace to my weary soul,
> That thou, my Lady are the angels' Queen.
> Shall I then fear
> To face the glittering ranks,
> That guard from steps profane,
> Heavens dazzling scene?
> Their flame tipped swords,
> Will lower at my cry:
> Angels of God, my Mother is your Queen!

Contemplation for Obtaining Love

In this meditation we come to the final object of life... the pure love of God. St. Ignatius concludes the *Spiritual Exercises* with this all important goal. He would have us bear in mind that real love is shown in deeds rather than in words. Love is the one subject that the world has been most interested in, but today the world seems further away from true love than ever before. This meditation brings to light the words of St. John, "My little children, let us not love in word, nor in tongue, but in deed and in truth" (1 John 3, 18).

The scene:

To see myself standing before God our Lord. His angels and saints are interceding for me.

The petition:

I shall ask for an interior knowledge of the many and great benefits I have received, that thoroughly grateful, I may in all things love and serve His Divine Majesty.

GOD'S GIFTS TO ME

In the "Foundation" I learned by reason that God created me and therefore has a right to my service. But since God created me for Himself, it is not only through love, but duty as well that I am to return my praise, reverence and service to Him. Here I shall reflect on God's gifts:

In my creation:

Had God not created me, I would simply be nothing. There may have been times in my life when I foolishly thought: Why did God create me? I did not ask to be brought into this world of trouble. But now I realize that I am here because of God's love and goodness. He had no need of creating me. He did so out of love. What shall I render to God for this gift of creation?

In my redemption:

Man sinned and thereby frustrated his purpose and end in life. But God still loved souls and sent His own Divine Son to redeem each and every soul. In the meditation on the Passion of Christ, I have seen to what extent love prompted His sufferings, crucifixion and death. God has a personal love for my soul.

In my daily life:

God has given to me all that I possess. He has given me a body with senses and a soul with faculties. He has given me this day and this hour. Above these natural gifts, He has given to me my faith, His sacraments and countless graces. What memories of His goodness and the guiding Hand of Providence my life affords!

How grateful I should be for my good parents, my education. How many times God has helped me in times of trouble, doubt and sin. Reflecting for a few moments on the past, I see that all were His special gifts to me. Indeed, these were His special marks of love.

What can I do for Him? It seems almost futile to think of a mutual interchange of love. But God does not think so. His invitation is always present and most sincere: "Child, give my thy heart."

"Take then, dear Lord, and receive all my liberty. Thou hast given me a certain amount, take it back and make me Thy servant. My memory, let me only use it for Thy service, for all that Thou mayest wish me to remember; my understanding, that I may be able to penetrate Divine things as deeply as Thou mayest desire; my will that I may be wholly thine. I only ask the favor of Thy love and grace."

GOD IS PRESENT IN ALL HIS GIFTS

We sometimes exchange pictures of our loved ones to keep them in mind although we really wish they were present. God is present in His gifts. He is present in the elements, giving them existence. He is present in the plants, giving them life. To the animals He gives sensation and instinct. But He dwells in a far nobler sense in man. I am His living temple where He can see His own image and find an intelligence capable of knowing and loving Him. What a wonderful truth! God present in me! Therefore, I am never alone. God is with me, and especially does He make His presence real when I receive Him in Holy Communion. Coming closer to God, what do I find to be true? I was in the mind of God from all eternity. Since creation He has sustained me in every beat of my heart, every thought, every prayer, every breath!

GOD ACTS IN ALL OF HIS CREATURES

God is not only present in His creatures, but He works in them. He works in order to give the plants their life, the lower creatures their instinct, man his intelligence. Nothing is done without the cooperation of God. He thinks of me every second of my life, not only the present, but the future, and He is continually planning for the best.

Why does God work in His creatures? It is all for me. In each one of His creatures that I may use, He is working for me. He is putting Himself at my disposal as a servant. He is doing what He did from the crib to the cross, "I am in the midst of you, as he that serveth" (Luke 22, 27). What is the particular significance? God wishes to show me that to love means to work, that love manifests itself in acts. If on every side I see God working for me, I must show my love in return by working for

Him, everywhere and in everything I do. I may work and be tired, but my love should never be tired.

Love for God is the motive I desire. Without love, or at least filial fear, I cannot praise, reverence and serve God, but with it ... I can become a saint. And this is God's will. With this thought I shall turn to the Sacred Heart of Jesus, the font of Love and pray to Him:

Be Thou in me, O Jesus, live in me, work in me, form and fashion me according to Your will, Your mysteries, Your actions and Your sufferings. You are the image of God; may I be the living image of Yourself; may I become like to You, as you wanted to be like to me in Your human nature; may I bear the effects and features of Your grace and Your glory. May Your birth make me be born anew; may Your childhood bring to me Your innocence; Your flight into Egypt make me flee the world and sin; may Your servitude render me Your servant; may Your bonds unloose me and deliver me from my sins, from my passions, from myself; may Your hidden and unknown life hide me from the world and vanity; may Your loneliness uphold me, Your temptations strengthen me, Your toils comfort me; may Your sorrow heal me, Your agonies hearten me, Your weariness console me, and may Your death make me live, reborn in eternity to share forever Your undying Love.

> "God has not promised skies ever blue,
> Flower strewn pathways
> All our lives through;
> God has not promised
> Sun without rain,
> Peace without pain.
> But God hath promised, dear friend,

Strength for the day,
Rest for the labor,
Light for the way,
Grace for the trials,
Help from above,
Unfailing sympathy,
Undying love."

My God I love Thee! In conclusion may these sincere words be constantly in my heart. May I teach others to look upward toward the Father in heaven. And may I in God's Providence be another shepherd of souls ever leading the flock to the one Adorable Shepherd—Christ the King, and Mary the Queen! Shepherd of my soul—I offer Thee my love now and forever. Amen.

APPRECIATION

This little book has come to you through the dedicated hands and hearts of the Fathers and Brothers of the Society of St. Paul. The members of this society are working today throughout the world to bring God's message of love and peace to as many as possible. In doing so, the special blessing of Pope Paul VI is with them each day and hour of their devoted service.

Kindly remember the Society of St. Paul in your prayers. They employ no outside help but do the publishing themselves.

If you are pleased with this little book could you order a copy for a dear relative or friend? If so, may the Good Shepherd reward you now and...always.

The author